I SPEAK ENGLISH

A Tutor's Guide to Teaching
Conversational English
Third Edition

By Ruth J. Colvin

Illustrations by Norman Mingo

 **LITERACY VOLUNTEERS OF AMERICA, INC.
SYRACUSE, NEW YORK**

All proceeds from the publication of this book go to further the work of Literacy Volunteers of America, Inc.

About the Author — Ruth J. Colvin, founder of Literacy Volunteers of America in 1962, has done extensive library, interview, and training research in her development of the versions of the text, **I Speak English** over the past 13 years. Colvin also has tutored students from many countries in conversational English, taken and given workshops and traveled extensively abroad. The recepient of three honorary doctorates, she holds a degree in Business Administration from Syracuse University.

About LVA — Literacy Volunteers of America, Inc. is a non profit, educational organization founded in 1962 in Syracuse, NY. Initially dedicated to training people to tutor adults and out-of-school teens to read and write, it added the conversational English training at the request of its tutors. In 1976, LVA developed an English Second Language Tutor Training Workshop and published the first edition of **I Speak English**. LVA has a nationwide network of affiliates and provides materials and services to many non-affiliated organizations, agencies, and individuals.

TABLE OF CONTENTS

INTRODUCTION

By 1776, America had welcomed newcomers from many countries with varied backgrounds and different languages. Two hundred years later, we still welcome newcomers who bring to North America their own rich cultures and languages. The United States of America was founded on the idea of accepting people from all over the world who would wecome the opportunity to work together in freedom, but a cooperative society needs common communication. To share the best that each can give requires thoughtful listening and effective speaking.

In North America the dominant language is English. To work, study, and function in America a person should be able to communicate in English.

Many individuals want to help our international guests and non-English speaking Americans communicate in English. Are there suggestions for these potential tutors? Are there specific useful techniques?

In this book I am pleased to share with you the best ideas that I have gleaned from many sources for helping others for whom English is a second languages. I have been accorded interviews with leaders in the field of English second language teaching, taken workshops and classes, done much reading in the professional literature, and used my own teaching to experiment. I have visited schools where English is taught as a second (or third, or fourth) language, not only in the United States, but also in the Soviet Union, South America, Turkey, Africa, Europe, the People's Republic of China, India, Burma, Thailand, Australia, and New Zealand.

Individuals who want to help someone learn conversational English (listening comprehension and speaking skills) need more than good will and enthusiasm, although these are important. Training in the "how to" skills can make the job easier and help to eliminate much unnecessary frustration. Awareness of the customs and cultures of newcomers to America, and a sensitivity to the feelings of these new neighbors can lessen tensions and help bring understanding and friendship.

This book is presented in a practical manner, so that volunteers with no previous teaching experience can teach effectively. You need only the ability to speak, read, and write in English, and a sincere desire to to teach one person.

This book does not claim original techniques. It was designed to be a simplified and condensed book of basic methods suggesting logical and helpful ideas for the person who is teaching English for the first time. Because of its basic approach, it has proven useful not only to the volunteer tutor, but also to paraprofessionals and professional teachers in other fields who have been called upon to teach conversational English. It is intended to be a resource to which you will want to refer again and again as you progress from being a beginning tutor to being an experienced one.

Chapters 1, 2, 3, 4 and 5 give important information which will help you know what to expect in working with the conversational English student. Chapters 6 through 13 present approaches, drills and activities from which you will be able to put together lessons which will help your student become proficient in listening, understanding and speaking English.

The techniques in this book are readily adaptable to small group instruction and Chapter 14 gives you suggestions for this.

The end matter is considered an integral part of the book. There you will find resource material which will help you prepare a practical sequence of lessons with your student. Topics covered there range from requirements for US and/or Canadian citizenship; a list of Recommended Books arranged by use; an adaptation of the Mainstream English Language Training resource package (MELT) which is a detailed guide to competency based topics for survival English; a bibliography of cited works on which this book was based; an informal placement test; to a list of suggested conversation starters.

There are classes in most cities for people who want to learn English as a second language, but even in such classes there are often students who need individual help. Too, there are students who lack the self-confidence to attend these classes and sometimes jobs interfere with the class time. In some areas, there are no English as a Second Language (ESL) classes.

For those who cannot attend classes, a trained volunteer tutor can fill a real need. Literacy Volunteers of America, Inc. (LVA) offers a six session workshop to train potential tutors, paraprofessionals, and professionals in proven techniques for teaching conversational English. **I Speak English** is the handbook that accompanies the LVA training.

I want to thank the many individuals who have helped by sharing their talents and time in the preparation of the earlier editions of this book. Sincere appreciation goes to: Shirley Botek, Frances Daly, June Dona, Doris Edie, Frances Singer Hennessy, Walter Lichtenstein, Carl Mattarochia, Thelma McPherson, Ellen Ossoff, Alice Perlman, Gloria Rasberry,Ph.D., Jane Root, Ph.D., Loretto Sadkin, Verna Scott, Thomas Sousa, Ph.D, and Helen Sumner.

A special thanks to those whose work has contributed to this third edition: Jeffery P. Bright, Linda Carl, Marcia Dean, Willy Evans, Wendy Jones, Kathy Kuy, Patrick Moran, Carol Smalley, and Alan Stern.

Robert Poczik, Associate in the Bureau of Continuing Education, New York State Department of Education,

Andrea Osburne, Ph.D., Assistant Professor, Central Connecticut State College, and C. Ray Graham, Ph.D, Professor, Department of Linguistics, Brigham Young University have served as consultants for LVA's total Conversational English training. Beulah Rohrlich, Ph.D., Professor, Syracuse University served as a consultant for the segment on Intercultural Communication in the workshop. I am most grateful to them for their helpful criticism and suggestions.

I am indebted to the late Norman Mingo who volunteered his professional talent to provide the drawings for **I Speak English**.

A special thanks to Virginia K. Lawson, Ph.D., LVA's Vice President, Publishing and Marketing for editing the third edition of **I Speak English**.

Thanks, also, to other LVA staff: Jinx Crouch, President; Jonathan McKallip, Vice Presdent of Field Services; and Barbara MacDonald and Chip Carlin, Editorial Assistants, for their comments.

To all those who shared their ideas at conferences, in training sessions, and in their books, thereby adding to my knowledge, as well as to the tutors and students who have given me joy and encouragement, I dedicate this book.

RJC
Syracuse, NY
August, 1986

CHAPTER 1

Language as Communication

Need for Communication in a Common Language...The Nature of Language... Nonverbal Communication

Most of our ancestors came to this country as foreigners. We like to think of them with nostalgia and fond memories. But what about the newly-arrived "foreigners"? They are often viewed with suspicion and mistrust — sometimes with pity and compassion — or perhaps with friendship and a helping hand.

You may know some Americans who reversed the process and lived a part of their lives on foreign soil. Many Americans have had the experience of visiting a country with a language strange to them and have temporarily experienced the feeling of "apartness" from the life around them. But these fellow countrymen had the security of knowing they would soon be back home, comfortable and able to cope in a familiar tongue.

But what of the thousands transplanted from their native lands who now live in the United States? A new language, often an immediate need to find employment, a different

life style, strange foods, unfamiliar government, homesickness for friends and family — all combine to make life very difficult indeed. These same people bring a rich heritage to their new homeland, but unless they can communicate, they cannot learn the "new" or share the "old".

Communication — the "reaching out" of one human being to another — is accomplished in various ways. We communicate nonverbally with our body movements, and we also communicate by listening, speaking, reading, and writing. Just how much of our time is spent in this business of communicating? According to an estimate by the New York State Department of Education, 70% of a person's waking time is spent in communicating. The average person spends 45% of this communication time listening, 30% speaking, 16% reading, and 9% writing. Obviously, these percentages vary with each individual, but unless we're eating or sleeping, we are communicating.

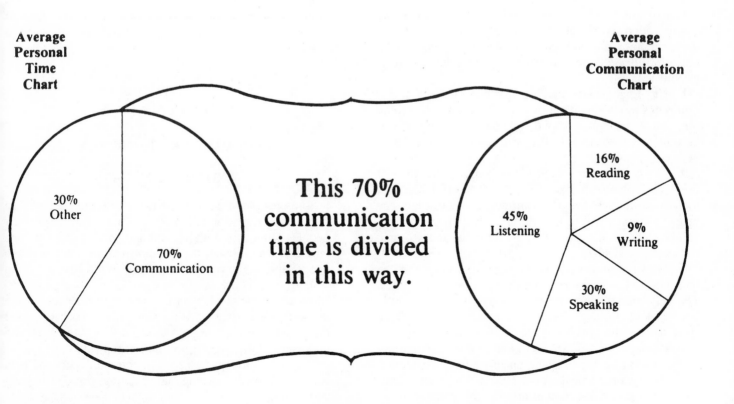

Average Personal Time Chart

30% Other

70% Communication

This 70% communication time is divided in this way.

Average Personal Communication Chart

16% Reading

45% Listening

9% Writing

30% Speaking

Need for Communication in a Common Language

A mouse and her three children were out for a leisurely stroll when suddenly they were confronted by a menacing cat. The mother mouse reacted quickly and shouted "Bow wow!" The cat fled. Turning to her children the mother mouse chided, "Now do you see the importance of learning a second language?" (Lit-Bits, 1975)

On the television series, "Upstairs, Downstairs" (produced by the British Broadcasting Company), there was an episode in which the Bellamy family takes in a refugee Belgian family at the beginning of World War 1. This Belgian family speaks only French, and the English household speaks only English.

The problems seem insurmountable:

1. The servants in the English household, in an effort to be hospitable, serve tea to their guests. The Belgians aren't sure what it is. They taste it — and spit it out!

2. The Belgians, after their travels, are very dirty and the English servants prepare a big bathtub for them, trying to indicate by gestures that they should bathe. The Belgians are indignant and refuse.

3. A small Belgian boy grabs a jar of jam and sits under the cook's table eating it with special pleasure. Mrs. Bridges, the cook, grabs for him but misses. The little boy drops the jam, laughs, and runs away. The Belgian family roars with laughter, much to the disgust of the English servants.

Utter chaos is near, with the Belgians acting more and more suspicious and the English servants ready to leave en masse. The head of the English household brings in a niece who has just returned from abroad and who speaks both French and English.

Her first act is to formally introduce the Belgians to the English servants, which is accepted by both. Then in a diplomatic way, she finds out the problems, for which there are obvious solutions as soon as communication is established.

1. The English are unaware that tea to the Belgians represents medicine. When it is given to them they think they are being poisoned and, of course, spit it out and become very suspicious. Coffee or hot chocolate would have been acceptable.

2. The Belgians very much wanted baths but they thought the English servants wanted them to undress and bathe right there with an audience. They were aghast. But when they realize that water will be brought in, a screen provided, and no one will be in the room, they are delighted and welcome the chance to bathe.

3. The English servants were upset by the laughter of the little boy as he ate the jam and dropped the precious jar. The Belgians explained that this was the first time the little boy had done anything mischievious or had enjoyed anything since the day he saw his father shot by the enemy. The Belgians were so relieved and pleased that their natural response was laughter. Empathy, understanding, and admiration follow. Communication is a must and without a common language, real communication is difficult.

Nature of Language

As tutors of English to speakers of other languages, we are primarily concerned with listening comprehension and the speaking of English, and our goal is to help our students to communicate in the language of their new country.

The primary purpose of language is communication, and we as teachers must help our students use the language, specifically English, to communicate. Anyone who cannot speak or understand the language is really cut off from the life of the community.

The skills of language acquisition begin with experience. In learning a language totally, there are four specific skills involved:

> listening
> speaking
> reading
> writing

Every person has internalized the **systems** of his/her native language (the basic patterns or structures of the language, i.e. the forms and arrangements of words, sounds, and meaning) while still very young. Most people are to perform two language skills in their own language: listening and speaking. Not everyone has the skills for reading and writing in their native language. If complete mastery of a language is desired, the listening and speaking skills are generally learned first. This is obvious, if you consider that:

1. Children understand and speak their native language before they learn to read and write.

2. Most people speak and understand their native language, even though many cannot read or write it.

Therefore, spoken language is generally considered the **primary** language system with the written as the **secondary** language system. If the primary system is learned first, reinforced by the secondary system, the problem of constantly translating (that so many of us had if we learned to read and write a foreign language before we learned to speak and understand it) can be avoided to a large extent.

PRIMARY LANGUAGE SYSTEM
is the
SPOKEN LANGUAGE

SECONDARY LANGUAGE SYSTEM
is the
WRITTEN LANGUAGE

Some people think that one cannot "know" a language if one cannot read it and write it. This is not true. Many peoples of the world understand and speak more than one language even though they cannot read or write a single one. (Some of the world's languages do not have a writing system). The converse also is true. Even though a person can read and write a language, that person may not be able to speak or understand it. How many Americans have passed their written French exam, but when they go to Paris can understand little, or are not understood?

Our goal is to help people gain communication skills in English, through listening and speaking, through reading and writing.

Before discussing ways to help your student, let's think more about the nature of language. What is it? As stated above, language is a system of meaningful sounds used to communicate. These sounds are meaningful because they are produced in a patterned way that is mutually understood by speakers of the same language.

Therefore, in order for communication to take place, both the speaker and the listener must know the four sub-systems inherent in every language. Each sub-system has its own set of "rules." The rules which govern the English systems are different from rules which govern another language's systems.

The sub-systems (based on Schwan,) are:

1. Sound
2. Vocabulary
3. Structure
4. Social Usage

We will discuss each sub-system separately.

1. *Sound* — To get a clearer idea of what it means to say that language is a system of meaningful sounds having pattern, think of these three kinds of *sounds:* (Poczik)

a. Noises in traffic or at a construction site: These are a jumble of sounds with no particular pattern or structure.

b. People talking in a foreign tongue: These sounds are understood by some people but perhaps not by you. The sounds follow a regular pattern and thus have structure. You just don't know the structure or the meaning of the sounds.

c. People conversing in English. These sounds are organized in such a way that you who know English structure and vocabulary can comprehend the meaning. This is communication for those of us who understand English.

One part of the sound system is the *phonic* system - that is, the individual sounds of the language. English has approximately 44 phonemes - vowels,(a,e,i,o,u); dipthongs, (double vowels like *oy, ow,* and *uy*) and 29 consonants (*b, c, d, f, g, h, j, k, l, m, n, p, q, r, s, t, v, w, x, y, z*)

Another important part of the sound system of a language is the way in which letters can go together. In English *bl* can begin a word but *ng* does not. Not all languages have

as many vowels or the same set of consonants or put letters (sounds) together in the same way. This difference might cause a problem for some students.

2. *Vocabulary* — One way meaning is conveyed is by words. When we know a word, we also know the rules for its acceptable use, occurrence with other words, and grammatical class. Even if we can't name the rule, as speakers of a language, we know whether or not a statement sounds right.

3. *Structure* (word order and grammar) — Another way in which meaning is conveyed in language. This means that the relationship between words is regular, patterned, and conveys meaning to other speakers of the same language. For example, *The dog chased the boy.* has meaning for speakers of English partially because of the order of the words. Because the noun *dog* comes before the verb *chased,* we know who is doing the chasing. Because of the pronunciation of the *d* on the end of *chased* we know that the action took place in the past. We could not know this until the vocabulary was set in a pattern or structure.

The way words are pronounced in a spoken sentence also follows rules of structure in order to convey meaning. This sub-system of rules connecting meaning with structure includes:

Stress — commonly called the accented syllable or syllable. "*Joe* drove the car home." (Not Bill or Bob). "Joe *drove* the car home." (He didn't push it or have it towed.) Stress in English resides on the main stem word — as *come becoming*

Juncture — "Weak cough." rather than "We cough."

Our comprehension of spoken English is largely dependent on the rhythm, intonation, and stress we hear. These areas are often difficult for new language learners to master. Providing correct models will help.

Listening to TV, radio, and to Americans talking will help your student get the "feel" or the "melody" of this new language. Here is where a tape recorder is most helpful since the student can take it home to use in repeated practice.

It takes much more than word knowledge to communicate effectively as Nila Magidoff discovered. She arrived in the USA from the Soviet Union and was asked to give a speech for the Russian War Relief organization. Her English was limited, but she optimistically said she would do it if they would give her two weeks. Two weeks? That seemed impossible — but she decided she could do it by writing down 50 words every day and learning them phonetically. Every day she learned 50 more words and every night she prepared a new list of 50 words. To help improve her pronunciation, she went to the movies, studied poetry, etc. She had not engaged a teacher because she felt she could move ahead faster on her own. She felt that if she knew the words, people would understand what she said, even though there would be grammatical errors. The big day arrived, and she gave the speech. She felt certain that her efforts had proven effective. What a disappointment it was when one man took her hand and said, "Thank you so much. I didn't understand a word you said, but it was all so beautiful." (Allen, Hall)

Nila Migidoff learned that the meanings we wish to communicate require not only words, but correct order and stress patterns as well.

5

4. **Social Usage** — Sometimes meaning is conveyed not by literal use but rather by custom, idioms, such as when talking about a *lemon* as a bad car, not as a piece of fruit.

In teaching English to non-native speakers we want to help them internalize all four of the SYSTEMS. We do this initially through the skills of listening and speaking. Reading and writing skills generally follow when more of the systems have been internalized. Don't be upset if students who are literate in their own language want to *see* the written words. This can be a reinforcement to them.

Nonverbal Communication

There is nonverbal communication all around us. Sometimes we are conscious of it, but often we are not. For example, imagine we are in a restaurant. I want more coffee and have a hard time getting the waitress' eye. She finally sees me. I lift my empty coffee cup. She nods, and then gestures, as though pouring cream, raising her eyebrows, suggesting a question. I shake my head. No verbal communication, but we've communicated. The waitress brings me coffee without cream.

Gestures may have different connotations in different cultures. One can be totally unaware of such nonverbal communications as the raised eyebrow or cocking the head. You and your student, unconsciously, are sending communication signals. It is helpful to you, as a tutor, to become aware of such signals by knowing more about your student's culture and by helping your student understand the American ways.

Music is another form of nonverbal communication. Recognition of a tune can bring a light to one's eyes, even though the words and the setting may be foreign. In Russia, I was in a church where everything was different — the language, the setting, the service. However, in the middle of the service, the congregation sang a hymn, in Russian, of course, but to a tune familiar to me. I sang along loudly in English, feeling we were communicating, certainly not in words, but in music.

Many students from other countries are vaguely aware of some American customs such as the handshake instead of a bow as a greeting. Some of our common gestures, including waving when departing, beckoning with a forefinger, putting a finger to our lips to ask for silence, smiling to show approval,or frowning and shaking the head to show disapproval are known to newcomers, but some of our gestures are not understood.

In order to test your own observance of nonverbal communication, watch a TV program, cutting off the sound. See if you can understand what is being said. Or, at a gathering or a party, stand back and observe the gestures of people without listening to their conversation. Watch how Americans use their hands and how close people stand to each other. Edward Hall, in his book *The Hidden Dimension* (1966) says, "We are often unaware that distances between people in the American society are significant." He suggests that there is an intimate zone, where people talk together, standing 18 inches apart. If someone invades this private area, there is a tendency to back away. If you're further apart, there is a tendency to move closer. Hall goes on to say, "There is a personal zone where people are from 1 and ½ to 4 feet apart, a social distance where they are 12 feet or more apart. This does not necessarily apply to other cultures." In Latin and middle Eastern countries the distances are shorter. In Asian countries, the distances are greater.

There are some very simple gestures that will be useful to you as your teach a non-English speaking person. Early in the teaching sessions, establish certain signals which convey definite instruction. These gestures may not be needed very long, especially if you reinforce them with the verbal "listen" or "repeat."

Language is useful to the degree that it is used to communicate, and helping to make that communication possible for those who speak little or no English is the purpose of the conversational English tutor.

CHAPTER 2

Profile of the Conversational English Student

North America was settled and built by immigrants. Except for native American Indians, the millions of people now living in the USA and Canada are immigrants or descendants of people born in foreign lands. The earliest immigrants, who were adventurers or explorers, were followed by men and women who saw the New World as a place for a better life. With the exception of slaves who came involuntarily, these people came to America for economic, political, or religious reasons. Wars, revolutions, religious persecutions, and poverty have brought millions of people to North America since 1607.

The Spanish, Portuguese, English, and French were followed by the Dutch, German, Irish, Swedish, and Scottish people. Since most of the colonies followed the English customs of law and government, English became the language of America.

Between 1890 and 1924, 20 million people arrived in America, not only from western and northern Europe, but from eastern and southern Europe, and from Asia:Slovaks, Hungarians, Serbs, Poles, Ukranians, Russians, Italians, and Asians. Subsequent waves immigration preceded and followed World War II as more Eastern Europeans, South Americans, people from the Caribbean islands and Asia came to North America.

Recently, thousands of refugees have joined the immigration — Cubans, Vietnamese, Cambodians, Russians, Haitians, Salvadorans, Nicaraguans, Laotians, Indians and Pakistanis.

Often immigrant communities of people with similar backgrounds have developed and currently exist in all major North American cities. Historically Swedes and other Scandinavians settled in Minnesota and the Dakotas. Many immigrants stay near their ports of entry: Cubans in Florida; Orientals in California or along the railroad lines across Canada; French in Quebec; Mexicans in Southern California or Texas. Immigrants, bringing with them a particular skill or trade, travel and settle in the place where their talents can be employed and where relatives and friends are already established in jobs. It is natural to go where one has friends and relatives, where someone understands one's customs and knows one's language.

People continue to come to America either to live or to visit or to study for a period of time. If they don't know how to speak and understand English, life here can be very difficult.

Juan Vargas came to the United States from Mexico to get a better job and find more opportunities for his family. He cannot speak or understand English. How can he venture out on a bus when he cannot ask directions or understand anyone? How can he apply for a job when he cannot communicate in English?

Mariko Yano is in Canada with her husband from Japan. Mr. Yano is doing graduate work at the university, but Mrs.Yano takes care of the house and family. How does she shop for food for her family when she speaks no English? Supermarkets allow her to pick out what she wants — and pictures on cans and packages certainly help. However, pictures can be misleading. Several students bought cat food thinking it was tuna because they couldn't read the English words and in their countries animal (pet) food is not sold in a market.

Huong Nguyen is a teenager from Vietnam. She speaks French and Vietnamese and has studied English for two years. She reads and writes English well and can speak some English. Her problem is understanding spoken English. It's a garbled mess to her because native English speakers speak so fast, and she has a real problem understanding teenagers who use idioms and slang. She can read and get information in school from her books, but she's at a complete loss when it comes to lectures and conversation with her peers.

Our concern as tutors is to help people communicate in English — to develop listening and speaking skills — conversational English. Our goal is to help speakers of other languages who cannot communicate in English enter the mainstream of American life.

Reasons for Learning English

It is helpful to know why your student wants to learn English. Conversational English students have specific motivations for language learning. For example:

1. They want to get jobs. Even a dishwasher needs to be able to follow instructions in English. An accountant from one country may find him/herself working as a maintenance person in the United States because he/she can't transfer job abilities to the English-speaking market.

2. They want to pass medical boards or take graduate courses. Often people who are well educated and can read and write English fluently need help in the verbal communication skills.

3. They want to make friends in this new country.

4. They need to be functional in their new country — to be able to go shopping, get to a doctor or a clinic, answer the telephone, listen to the radio and TV, and enjoy American movies.

5. They want to become citizens and need help to pass the citizenship test.

6. They want to be able to speak English with the younger members of their family. Older students who cannot speak

English often are embarrassed and ashamed because the young people in their household only want to speak English.

If you can understand an individual's reasons for wanting to learn, you can zero in on helpful ideas.

NEED FOR FRIENDSHIP AND ACCEPTANCE

Most of us are so involved in our own daily lives that we forget there are people living in the community who really need to be accepted as neighbors and friends, not just allowed to live nearby. This is illustrated in the following incident.

Two travelers stopped at a small diner for a sandwich. The woman and the two men working there had charming foreign accents. Conversation brought out the fact that they were Greek, had been in the United States for six years, had some family back in Greece, and had found America wonderful. They had become citizens and were proud of it — but they couldn't understand many of the American ways.

They wanted and needed someone to explain and discuss with them American holiday customs, politics, schools, and parent organizations. All their associations were within the family, and it was difficult for them to become part of an American community. They felt they couldn't take the initiative. Invitations to American homes would have been most welcome.

As Americans, we can and should become sensitive to the need for friendship and acceptance of the "stranger in our midst" and in so doing, we enrich ourselves and our own lives.

NEED FOR A JOB

People who cannot read or understand English may have difficulty in finding a job no matter how impressive their other qualifications may be. Many newcomers have college and advanced degrees in medicine, engineering, or law, but are unemployable until they learn conversational English. Their talents often are not evident because they cannot be expressed.

At the other end of the scale, many people come to America because they have had no opportunity for education or upward mobility in their native lands. Before they can apply for most jobs, they have a real need for conversational English.

Anticipated Progress

There are several things which affect how quickly people might learn to speak English: aptitude, motivation, opportunities to learn, the amount of knowledge that a person begins with, as well as reinforcement from his/her environment. You will want to take these into consideration as you informally evaluate your progress.

If your student speaks no English and can understand nothing you say at first, be patient. If you start simply and build slowly, little successes will bring a flash of comprehension when understanding does come. If you are the first person with whom your student can communicate in English, you have become a very important person in his/her life in this country. As you encourage your student to use new found English skills with others, the good feelings which come with success will multiply.

If, on the other hand, your student already speaks some English, even though haltingly, with a heavy accent and some of what you say can be understood, your progress can be more rapid than with an absolute beginning student.

Do not be discouraged if your student reaches a plateau and does not seem to be progressing. This is quite common in language learning, often preceding the next big improvement.

Barriers to Progress

ABILITIES AND BACKGROUNDS

Tutors will encounter students of widely differing abilities among those to whom English is a second language. The individual who has had adequate background in a language other than his/ her mother tongue will be far easier to teach than the person whose verbal experience is poor in any language. For him or her, only a transfer process is required. It will be easier for someone who speaks a Romance language and/or uses the Roman alphabet to learn English than someone from a background using other alphabets such as Arabic or Chinese.

If we take into consideration ability and background, there are four categories of students. Knowing which description fits your student will help you understand his potential rate of learning.

1. The person who is illiterate in any language and does not understand or speak English.
2. The person who is literate in his/her own language, but who cannot read, write, understand or speak English.
3. The person who can understand, speak, read and write in his/her native language and one or more other languages, but not English.
4. The person who can read and write in English very well, and may speak, read, and write several languages, and who understands and speaks some English.

FEAR OF EMBARRASSMENT

Students will often hesitate to *try* speaking English because they fear making mistakes. If you start slowly and work quietly, with no outsider to hear errors, you can instill confidence in your student.

BEHAVIORAL PATTERNS

Often the non-English speaking person is shy and scared. Knowing a few words, such as *Hello* and *Thank you,* aren't enough to last through a community meeting or a session at the employment agency. And when one needs help in an emergency, it can be a frightening experience not to be able explain what is wrong!

Other non-English speaking persons might seem loud and boisterous, a defense mechanism to cover up a lack of confidence. People react to stress in many different ways.

DIFFICULTY WITH SOME SOUNDS

Even immigrants with excellent educations often have difficulty in *speaking* the English language. It is important to realize that the ability to make certain sounds characteristic of spoken English may be a major difficulty to some foreign speakers because these sounds are not included in their language.

Each language has a sound system peculiar to that language. To learn to speak another language often involves a whole new set of musclular movements to make the appropriate sounds.

COMPREHENSION PROBLEMS

Even for the student who can read and write English (having studied its structure) the problem often is understanding *spoken* English (listening comprehension) and having the ability to speak it. Native English speakers use many contractions and often join words together. Don't many of us say, "Wha-cha-do-n" when we mean "What are you doing?" It is difficult to slow down and separate words distinctly.

There are idioms peculiar to each language and culture and many idioms in English-speaking America are often most frustrating and incomprehensible. Much patient help is needed here.

Highly Motivated Students

Generally, the highly motivated student is not only a willing student but most persistent, and will often learn quickly. The desire and the need to learn the new language is often a spur to learning. The real motivation may be the need to understand lectures at the university, or to communicate with younger members of a family who speak English fluently, or the need to communicate better in the working world.

Motivation to learn and academic success depend not only on innate ability, but also to a great extent, on whether an individual wants to learn and feels capable of learning.

There are two kinds of motivation: instrumental and integrative. In instrumental motivation, the individual wants to learn the second language for personal gains (jobs, reading, travel) but not to be like the group. In integrative motivation the individual desires to learn the second language in order to communicate, interact and become part of a community. A person learns a language better if he or she is learning it for integration purposes.

Whoever your student is, whatever her/his origin, whatever abilities or weaknesses are evident, you must be sensitive to the individual's real needs. Using the "how to" skills which you will learn, together with your own attributes, you can help at least one person to communicate in English and live a fuller life.

CHAPTER 3
Profile of the Good Tutor

Training...Planning...Personal Qualities

In all history, it is **individuals** who makes the difference — sometimes for good and sometimes for evil. So, don't underestimate the potential of each individual. Don't underestimate your own influence, even in regard to one person. You may be a professional teacher, an expert in some other field, an engineer, or a homemaker. You may be just the person to teach someone who wants to learn to understand and speak English.

Whatever your previous training, some of the skills you already have will help you to learn the new skills you need. Some of these skills are mechanical — practical methods for teaching English — but of equal importance are patience, enthusiasm, creativity and adaptability as well as respect for your student.

Training

How can you prepare yourself to tutor someone to speak and understand English? The desire to help and the willingness to give time are not enough. Even an ability to speak your student's language won't suffice. Learning the skills and techniques of teaching English as a second language and making well-thought-out lesson plans are essential to a good tutor.

Literacy Volunteers of America, Inc. offers training in tutoring Conversational English. The training is a professionally designed and field-tested workshop. The workshop is especially designed for the non-professional whose field is other than English as a second language but is used by professionals in the field as well. *I Speak English* is the handbook which accompanies this workshop. Together, they are designed to give you the needed skills and practice.

Other workshops and college courses teaching conversational English are offered in many communities. In addition to the Literacy Volunteers of America workshop, these other training opportunities increase one's skill at helping someone learn to speak English.

Planning

As a volunteer tutor, you are responsible for teaching, for planning your student's lessons, and for keeping records.

Your main job is to help your student grow in listening comprehension and speaking skills, and each session with your student must be just that — a teaching session. Because there never seems to be enough time for everything you anticipate doing, plan your lesson well. Make the most of your time together, keeping a good mixture of review, new learning, and fun. Often after concentrating on the lesson and

meeting some success from the challenge, a student can view a personal problem with new hope.

Personal Qualities

PATIENCE

Good tutors have many virtues, but perhaps the greatest of these is patience. Sometimes learning may seem very slow, but there are times when all the carefully built knowledge seems to come to gether all at once, and the student suddenly says, "Oh, I see." Then all the patient work becomes worthwhile and the joy of learning is realized for both tutor and student.

UNDERSTANDING

Because conversational English students cannot speak English, many of them have had great problems in finding a place to live, getting a job, even being functional in everyday ways. They may have found it hard to use local transportation, to buy food, to get help in an emergency. You are not expected to solve every problem, but perhaps you can steer your student to someone who can help. You certainly can respect them as adults who have real problems because they can't communicate in English. The fact that your students are adults is most important. To be treated as a child can be very degrading and the tutor should avoid any hint of suggestion of such treatment.

ADAPTABILITY

People are infinitely different. Some have phenomenal memories; others have keen intuition; some have a knack of learning through observation; and some are patient plodders who will learn in time if you have patience enough to allow that time. Your job is to adapt your teaching to your student's interests and abilities. Be open-minded to new ideas and plan a variety of teaching techniques.

ENTHUSIASM AND ENCOURAGEMENT

Keep your enthusiasm high, giving genuine encouragement to your student. A feeling of achievement with small successes must occur before any long-term success can be achieved. However, do not pretend success when both of you know that it is not deserved. Excessive excitement and urging are not conducive to learning, but genuine respect and regard for the student's growth can be sources of help and pride. Give encouragement, not only as to progress in lessons, but also in your student's participation in community activities. Suggest that listening to TV and radio programs can be good practice in hearing and understanding the spoken language as well as contributing much information.

Remind your student that participation in small group conversations is helpful, and that classes are available for further study and reinforcement.

SENSE OF HUMOR

A tough task is often made easier by including some light moments. Laughter often reduces tension and a good joke shared is a fine way to build a relationship and to add pleasure to some otherwise hard work. A teaching hour with several laughs in it will seem like a much shorter time. An occasional mistake (perhaps in pronouncing a word in your student's language) makes more legitimate the mistakes your student makes. It is not so bad to be wrong, and sometimes tutors are wrong. When you laugh, be sure your student is laughing with you. Remember, adults can be very sensitive, especially in areas where they feel insecure and inadequate.

SENSITIVITY

There is a need for a tutor of conversational English to be sensitive to what a student is facing. The best way might be to have lived in another country without knowing the language of that country. Some tutors may have come to the United States as immigrants and do understand some of the very real problems, frustrations, and dreams of these newcomers. But most of us have not had this experience and must try to gain empathy by reading, observing, and studying our students and by being aware of both verbal and nonverbal interactions between an American tutor and a non-English speaking student.

Verbal language is indeed an important part of total communication, but nonverbal language may make up the larger part of the communication process.

Often we tend to assume that someone who does not speak our language does not know much about the customs of our country. In contrast, we may assume that someone who speaks our language also knows and understands our customs. In order to help a student, it is important to explain some of the cultural systems in America. Little things are too often taken for granted, and these must be shared with your student.

For example, in the United States, when you are invited for dinner, you can arrive five or ten minutes later than the time set, never an hour late and never early. However, if you have an appointment for a job interview, you should be at least five minutes early. American time standards do vary.

Sometimes a woman may offer her hand when being introduced but sometimes she will simply nod and say, "How do you do?" or merely say, "Hi!" on meeting someone. Men more generally greet with a handshake. Teenagers greet each other more casually. Your student will need to know how to recognize the occasion for each behavior. Much will depend on the relative social status or age, gender, or on the circumstances of the moment. Try practicing with your student in a role-playing situation.

Cultural understanding of time and space (the distances people stand between each other in a conversation) are important. Even more advanced conversational English students may not understand cultural differences and need to be taught. Your student will appreciate your sensitive help.

Knowing the customs of your student's country will help you find contrasts as well as similarities with customs in our own country. One set of behaviors is not better than another, just different. A person is likely to be more comfortable and more easily accepted if the customs of the adopted country are known.

CREATIVITY

To be creative in teaching conversational English may be difficult until you have a knowledge of basic techniques. But once you feel comfortable with basics, the next step toward creativity is easier. Then, all the techniques can be adapted to individual needs and individualized instruction. This book encourages tutor creativity. Individualized lessons are most effective when you use the basic techniques as a springboard to creative endeavor. Use your own imagination as your confidence in your teaching skills increases. Don't overlook conversational English textbooks. Creatively used they can be an excellent basis for instruction.

RESPONSIBILITY

Success stories are stimulating, but not all students are equally successful. Some are highly motivated to learn English, others easily retreat into their native language. Your responsibility is to be prepared to face some of the more common problems conversational English students have and not to judge yourself too harshly if your student doesn't respond to your efforts.

AWARENESS OF SPECIAL PROBLEMS

There are special problems that cause some people to learn more slowly than others. Some students need considerable repetition; others absorb and remember everything. Whatever the ease or difficulty of learning, treat your student as an individual with due allowance for differences in rate and style of learning. If your student does join a conversational English class, see that you coordinate your work with that of the professional teacher. Reinforcing class sessions should be a major part of your lesson plans. In any event, good working relations between a tutor and a classroom teacher are important.

Be concerned about the total person of your student. Working on a one-to-one basis, you may be confronted with real problems for which you do not have the answers. Be ready to refer your student to appropriate agencies for help. As conversational English tutors, we have an ideal opportunity to tell other Americans about the problems and capabilities of foreign-born students, so others can understand and help in real ways. You can not only learn about your student's culture, but you can also share this information with your friends. The ethnic majority should know about the ethnic minorities who live within their community.

COMMITMENT

A good volunteer makes a real commitment to the job. Your work will result in influencing at least one person's life. A teaching commitment requires:

1. **Training** — Mastering techniques for teaching English as a second language.

2. **Planning** — Setting long and short range goals with your student and writing out lesson plans which will work towards those goals.

3. **Dedication** — Teaching at least one student for two one-hour sessions (minimum time) each week for a minimum of 50 hours.

4. **Accountability** — Keeping progress records, and reporting to your sponsoring organization.

Getting to know **one** person from another country, with different customs and with a different native language, helps expand each person's awareness of the great variety of human experience. The one person you meet represents that country and its customs to you. You may be the only North American your student gets well acquainted with, and accordingly, you represent a "typical American" or a "representative Canadian" to your student. Quite a challenge for both of you!

CHAPTER 4

Other Cultures

Definition of Culture...Cultural Preconceptions...Sharing Our Own Culture... Learning About the Student's Culture... Some Cultural Differences... Respect for Other Cultures

The elements and skills of language plus culture equals natural and effective communication. Words have meaning only in the context of the culture in which they are used. For example, a *bonnet* is the hood of the car in England, but in America a *bonnet* is a head covering. Learning about a new culture does not mean giving up another culture. But as we learn a new language, learning the culture is important. Language learning and culture learning cannot be divorced.

Definition of Culture

Culture is a system of behaviors and beliefs making some things permissible under certain circumstances and nearly prohibiting them in others. These patterns of culture may vary from country to country and from area to area. What may be normal or acceptable in one part of the world may be frowned upon in another. A culture is defined by the human behavior that is accepted by the majority in that particular community. Culture touches all aspects of language and communication. There is no doubt that culture and language are interrelated.

Cultural Preconceptions

We are products of our culture, and many of our ideas often result from cultural bias. This causes stereotyping. A stereotype is an idea of how *everyone* in a certain group looks or acts. Stereotypes are usually too general and too simple. Often, they're not very attractive. Few people fall into the "typical" picture. Members of other cultures are as individual as members of our own.

We may imagine Africans as living only in tribal villages. Many Africans live in towns and cities very similar to ours and have never lived in a tribal village or heard a tribal drum.

Similarly, people in other lands may have pre-conceived ideas about life in the USA. When they think of the culture of the United States, they may envision gangsters on every street corner and American Indians still engaged in buffalo hunting. Canadians are often seen as panning for gold in the Yukon, or trapping bear near Hudson Bay. Movies have given rise to the misconceptions that all Americans either live in the lap of luxury or are slum dwellers.

It is difficult to know what part of a person's attitudes is influenced by background and culture and what part by reading, learning, and various experiences.

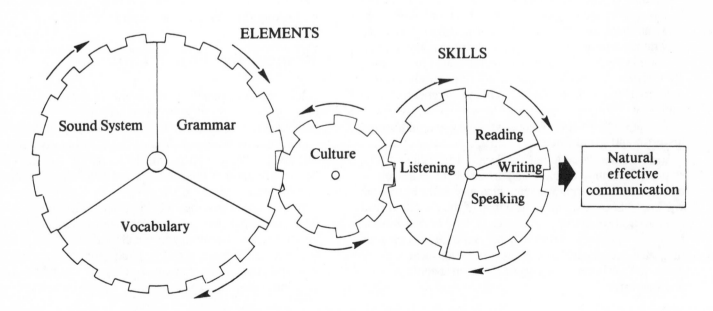

Chart from *Teaching English as a Second Language: A Self-Instructional Course, Unit 1 - The Nature and Purpose of Language.* Albany, NY: State Education Department, 1974.

Sharing Our Own Culture

People who are new to America or Canada want to know more about our ways and as tutors we have a responsibility to provide this information. Helping our students learn and understand North American customs, manners, holidays and attitudes certainly should be included as we plan lessons. It is important to convey to your student some of the general attitudes of Americans such as the near equality of the sexes, the fact that a majority of women work outside the home with the whole-hearted support of their husbands, and children have comparative freedom. However, do have empathy for your student. As Americans or Canadians we are rightfully proud of our country and customs, but we must not imply that our way is the only way.

Learning About the Student's Culture

However, many of us are uninformed of the customs, cultures, and often the geographical location of other countries. As you learn new perspectives and interesting facts from your student, you will become more attuned to your student's individual feelings and needs.

Learning a new language and trying to adapt to a new culture is a difficult task, and it can be frustrating. It is important that as a Conversational English tutor you are able to empathize with your student. Becoming acquainted with your student's native country and culture will build the needed rapport between you and your student. Such interest on your part is a courteous gesture and indicates a sincere interest in your student as a person. With a little knowledge you can avoid unknowingly offending anyone.

Cultural and family differences vary in North America from one section to another as they do within every country. Consider the difference in living styles among a rural Saskatchewan family, a well-to-do New York City family, a suburban family, a ghetto family, and a western ranch family. Also, there are religious differences within other countries, as there are in America, so it is difficult to make generalizations about an entire country on any matter. Because individuals, even within a given country or culture, are *individuals,* your student may not fit precisely into the mold ascribed to most people from a given country. Your student will forgive your lack of knowledge of his or her ways, but it is a gesture of good will to try and understand his ways and avoid offense.

You are encouraged to read books and articles about your student's country, culture, and language to help you to discover the interesting ways in which they differ from what you know. Look at an up-to-date map of the area, and read a modern novel about his culture, preferably one written by a native. Back issues of the *National Geographic* magazine are invaluable for information on nearly every country. Your library can suggest books on specific peoples and countries.

Some Cultural Differences

It would be impossible to detail all cultural differences but you should be sensitive to the fact that differences exist.

Greetings vary from culture to culture. The American, "Hi", "How're ya?" or a wave of the hand indicate an informal friendliness. In some cultures it is polite to be more formal and inquire about the health of each member of the family. Handshaking is common in many cultures, but it is often done differently. Sometimes it is firm and brisk, again limp and relaxed. Others grab the thumb and wrist with a hearty greeting. In some Asian cultures the custom is to place the hands together, giving a slight bow.

Anglos have a non-touching culture, while Latins tend toward a touching culture. Latins greet each other with hugs, kisses, and handshakes, while Anglos greet each other with a possible handshake, but generally with just, "Hello", and no touching.

Facial expressions convey different meanings in different cultures. Surprise or shock in the American culture is often shown by opening the eyes wide and raising the eyebrows. To a Chinese, this is often a sign of anger while to a Puerto Rican, it can be a sign of lack of understanding.

As was mentioned earlier, actual physical distances between people are determined by culture. People from some parts of the world, especially Latin America, like standing close. In conversation with an American, the Latin may feel chilled and consider him aloof because of the distance apart. An American may feel stifled by the closeness.

In many cultures great emphasis is put on hospitality. Sharing food is an important way of showing friendship and gratitude. In cultures where the extended family is a way of life, any relative, no matter how distant, has the right to ask for extended hospitality.

A teacher is held in high regard in most countries. Sometimes this attitude is so exaggerated that a student feels the teacher is *always* right and knows *all* the answers. Respect is often shown by casting eyes downward rather than by looking directly into the eyes of the teacher.

Respect for Other Cultures

It is important that the tutor never belittle the foreign way of doing things. Avoid value judgements when dealing with cultural differences. Instead, your interest in your student's culture is very essential. You'll find it fun to taste native dishes of other countries and to learn the customs and holidays of another land. One is not better than the other, just different.

If you are conscious of the importance of cultural understanding as well as the mechanics of English, you are on your way to becoming an excellent tutor. You will also find yourself a more sensitive adult. And this sensitivity will spill over into other areas of your day-to-day life, enriching all your experiences.

CHAPTER 5

Testing (A Guide to the Tutor)

Background Information...Explanation of Test Levels...Teaching Plans Indicated by Test Results...Conversational English Student Biographical Inventory

Background Information

Before you start teaching, you should have information on your student's background. This should include the data outlined on the Conversational English Student Biographical Inventory at the end of this section. This information is usually collected during an intake interview with the student prior to matching with a tutor.

Explanation of Test Levels

As with all teaching, you do not want to start too far above or below your student's level of ability. First, determine whether your student speaks and understands no English, is fairly independent in the use of English, or is somewhere in between.

The **English as a Second Language Oral Assessment (ESLOA)** test (Coye, et al) published by Literacy Volunteers of America, is a diagnostic instrument which will develop a student profile, measure the things already known and define areas where learning has not yet occurred. The assessment also shows areas where instruction is needed and can be used to measure progress. The results will place the student into one of four levels.

Level One tests the student's ability to listen and understand, using the identification of specific vocabulary items. No oral response is necessary.

Level Two uses basic survival vocabulary in elementary English structures. Oral responses in English are required.

Level Three requires informational answers and deals with simple grammatical structures. Responses in complete sentences are encouraged.

Level Four utilizes much more complex grammatical structures and requires answers in complete sentences.

There is an appendix which provides students with an opportunity to demonstrate their verbal ability in English without being restricted to specific pictures or manipulation of syntax.

The same test may be used as a post-test provided that approximately six months have passed since the initial testing.

Teaching Plans Indicated by Test Results

Test results provide valuable information for the development of lesson plans appropriate for your student. The Suggested Lessons following each level of the ESLOA provide ideas for grammatical structures and survival topics which will form the basis for a natural progression in language learning. The following chart visually presents a general plan to use in designing your lesson.

	Conversation (Listening and Speaking)	Reading as Reinforcement	Independent Reading and Writing
Levels 0-1	X		
Level II	X	X	
Levels III-IV	X	X	X

Levels 0-I — Work only on conversational English, the listening and speaking skills, as directed in this book.

Level II — Work mainly on conversational English (listening and speaking skills). However, you can reinforce words the student has heard, understood and spoken, by showing the student those words in print. We suggest *only* those words heard, understood and spoken be seen in writing or in print.

Levels III and IV — Adapt the conversational techniques to the student's individual needs. More help will probably be needed in pronunciation, listening with understanding to practical and possibly technical English (radio broadcasts, lectures, or committee meetings, where many voices are heard). Material that the student has heard, understood, and spoken can be readily introduced as reading material for reinforcement. Independent reading can be used as a basis for discussion.

An informal Conversational English Placement Test is included in Appendix F. It is especially helpful when a quick placement of a group of students is needed.

Unless your student speaks excellent, standard English with complete comprehension, you can assume your student wants and needs help in speaking and understanding. If the real needs are not *listening comprehension and conversation* (even though at an advanced level) but are *learning to read and write* English, you might want to refer that student to someone trained in teaching basic reading, or get some tools to help you teach basic reading. One such tool is LVA's **TUTOR — Techniques used in the Teaching of Reading** (Colvin, Root, 1984).

It's helpful to know if your student can read and write in his/her native language. If this information has not been given to you, simply ask your student if he can write in his native language and to give you a sample. Of course, you can't evaluate the quality but at least you will know if he/she can write at all.

Some students can read and write English but have much trouble with the listening and speaking skills. Ask your student to read and write for you in English. You can use the **READ** test (Colvin, Root, 1982) published by Literacy Volunteers of America, to determine the level of his/her reading skills.

LITERACY VOLUNTEERS OF AMERICA, INC.
Student Biographical Inventory

_____   _____
Affiliate   Date form completed

_____
Student's Name   Address   Tel. No.

Contact date _____ Date tutoring started _____ ESLOA Level _____

Program: Student in school _____ ABE _____ Corrections _____ Migrant _____
        Industry _____ Hospital _____ Library _____ General _____

Sex: M _____ F _____

Age: Under 15 _____ 15-20 _____ 21-30 _____ 31-40 _____ 41-50 _____ 51-60 _____ 60+ _____

Ethnic background:

   Country of birth: United States _____ Canada _____ Other (specify) _____

   Native Language (specify) _____ Other Languages _____

   Read & write_____ Read & write_____

   If born elsewhere, number of years in U.S. _____

Family background:

   Marital status _____ No. of children _____

   Other dependent family members _____

Educational background:
   If educated in American schools, circle highest level completed:

   Elementary 0 1 2 3 4 5 6 7 8   high school 1 2 3 4   college 1 2 3 4   post college (specify) _____

   If educated in another country, indicate age at leaving school _____

Years of study of English (if any) _____

Employment status:

   Profession or job skills _____

   Employed part-time_____ full-time _____

   Unemployed seeking _____ not in the job market _____

Specify any significant handicaps which might affect learning:

   Physical _____

   Mental _____

Time available for tutoring _____ Suggested place for tutoring _____

Referred by: _____

Name of tutor: _____

(Put additional information on back of this sheet.)

(This page may be duplicated for easy use.)

CHAPTER 6
Getting Started

Essential Questions...Modeling the Spoken Language...Student Survival Kit

Essential Questions

There are certain questions that beginning tutors most often ask which when answered help set the tone and content of the lessons. Included in the following answers are some practical tutoring suggestions.

IS THERE A NEED TO KNOW THE STUDENT'S LANGUAGE?

One question continually arises in regard to tutoring limited English-speaking students: How important is it for the tutor to speak and understand the student's native language?

Most tutors will not know the student's native language and it is not necessary that the tutor have this knowledge. Knowing some words in the student's native language **can** be useful for explaining a difficult concept or giving directions but it can also be a crutch that a tutor leans on instead of effectively teaching English. Often when the student and tutor cannot communicate in English, they revert to the student's language. This then adds the additional step of translation to the communication process.

This does not mean that you should avoid your student's language completely. There are obvious advantages — the quick help in explaining an abstract term and the security of sharing a common language. The use of a bilingual dictionary (English and your student's native language) is very helpful, providing your conversational English student is literate in his/her native language. It might be time-consuming to spend ten minutes attempting to act out the meaning of a difficult word like "develop" or "justice" when you can look it up in a bilingual dictionary at once. But in trying to learn English words, it is often more beneficial to the student if the teacher can demonstrate the meaning, and the student usually will remember the word longer.

When it is possible to illustrate a meaning through actions, gestures, pantomime, objects or pictures, by all means do so. Two purposes will be served. Your student will be helped to *think* in English, rather than to think in another language and then translate into English, and the impression will be far more lasting. In teaching conversational English, *use the student's native language as a last resort.*

There is a close tie between a person's language and culture, and while you do not want to emphasize your student's language, you should encourage conversation about your student's native country. Ask about customs, food, dress, and climate. You will find yourself learning more about a foreign land than many seasoned travelers know! If your questions are similar in structure to the ones you've taught previously, the discussion can be in simple English and your student will be using the newly-learned language about topics that are meaningful. Also, the student will enjoy speaking about his/her country and will welcome a chance to talk.

SHOULD I CORRECT THE STUDENT'S PRONUNCIATION?

New tutors of oral language skills are often overly concerned about correcting the student's pronunciation of English words. Pronunciation problems can basically be ignored at first, unless the student cannot be understood. If a student pronounces a word incorrectly, give the correct pronunciation, asking for it to be repeated. Then use the word correctly in a sentence. If, after several tries, the student still has difficulty with certain sounds, don't belabor the point, but try to determine which sounds are causing the trouble.

Remember, before your student can make a correct sound, the sound must be heard and recognized when contrasted with similar sounds. The sequence of learning requires that the sound be *heard* distinctly, then *identified* so that attention can be focused on the sound to be learned, then produced correctly. Often the sequence must be followed more than once before a sound is heard.

Because a student doesn't have a particular English sound in his/her native language, there is often difficulty even hearing it, much less saying it. Therefore, extra attention should be given to the listening discrimination stage of pronunciation learning. (See under "minimal pairs" below).

It is usually helpful to show your student how to form the sound instead of just asking for an imitation. For example, if your student cannot make the "th" sound, suggest putting the tongue between the teeth. Demonstrate the method by making the sound yourself, or use a mirror so that the student can "see" the mouth's shape and the tongue's position.

Adults often have a great difficulty with the very small muscular movements of speech when these movements are not contained in their native language. The guttural sounds in German, the nasal sounds in French, and the clicks of some African languages, are examples of sounds that the English language does not have. Some of the sounds in English are as difficult for many non-English speaking students to produce.

You might want to keep a list of words regularly mispronounced. Don't let the student see the spelling of a word until that word can be pronounced. You probably will soon note a pattern of pronunciation problems.

Don't expect your student to overcome a foreign accent easily or completely. Articulation in another language is a most difficult skill for most adults to acquire, and many accents have a special charm.

However, it is important to hear and to be able to reproduce sounds correctly. "I spik Inglis" can become "I speak English" with practice.

Many words have an entirely different meaning when only one sound is changed. *Sin* is much different in meaning from *seen*, *tin* from *teen*, *fill* from *feel*. When communication is distorted by mispronunciation , it is important for the student to understand that the result of the distortion is often a change of meaning.

The Spanish-speaking person will often have difficulty with the English "v". Those from other language backgrounds have trouble with the "th" sound. One student said "bocketbook" for "pocketbook." He needed help in differentiating between the sounds of "p" and "b" which have only slight muscular differences.

Minimal Pairs

You might use minimal pairs to show the importance of correct vowel or consonant sounds in English. Minimal pairs are two words which differ in only one sound, e.g. *seat*, *sat; bet, pet*. Select a group of word pairs that provide examples of the same contrast,i.e. for "p" and "b".

pill — bill	pail — bail
pie — buy	pair — bear
pest — best	

When you make up a list of minimal pairs for your student, use familiar words to keep the drill meaningful. Keep these minimal pairs in order at first. Later mix them up and see if your student can hear the differences.

At first tell your student not to vocalize these sounds. Suggest only listening discrimination, trying to identify the "p" and "b" sounds. Your student could raise one finger when he/she hears the "p" sound and two fingers when he/she hears the "b" sound, or you might write "p" and "b" and have the student point to the appropriate letter.

The next step is helping your student to produce one of the sounds. Have the student repeat after you:

T	S
pill	pill
pie	pie
pest	pest
pair	pair

To help your student understand that these small sound differences are meaningful, put the contrasting sounds into different sentences and contexts.

"Where's the pill? I have to take it now."

"Where's the bill? I have to pay it now."

Then give the student the first sentence, seeing if he/she can give you the correct response. A correct answer means the student can now hear the difference between the two sounds!

T — "Where's the pill?"

S — "I have to take it now."

T — "Where's the bill?"

S — "I have to pay it now?"

Next reverse roles — let the student give the first sentence, and *you* give the response. If you give the one expected, the student will know the sounds correctly.

As with much of teaching a language, you will need to observe your student and use common sense in deciding how much of a particular lesson needs to be spent on any one point. Remember to model the correct pronunciation and reward anything that comes close to correct, gradually moving the student to an accent which can be understood by others. You might want to notice how well others understand your student either by observing him/her when you are on field trips or by having him/her record something during a lesson and asking someone else how well they understand what is being said. This will help you remain objective about your student's progress. The more we hear other people's accents, the easier it is for us to understand them. We need to be sure that the students are speaking better, not just that we are understanding them better!

SHOULD I TEACH IDIOMATIC ENGLISH OR FORMAL ENGLISH?

An idiom is a succession of words whose meaning is not obvious through knowledge of the individual meanings of the constituent words but must be learned as a whole, e.g. *give way, in order to, be hard put to do it*. Because they are so common in all languages, and are necessary to understanding everyday English, they must be taught. Along with teaching idioms, you will have to teach when their use is appropriate — the more formal the situation, the less acceptable the use of idiom.

When Dr. Juan Flavier was trying to know the people of the Philippines better, so that he could teach them, he found that it was just as important to know their idioms as to know their language.

One day a farmer asked if he wanted "kisses honey." He declined because he wasn't sure what was meant. His colleague accepted, and the farmer opened an old biscuit tin. It contained shredded tobacco and cigarette paper. Then the meaning became clearer. The farmer put some tobacco on the rectangular paper, rolled it expertly, and licked the edge to keep it in place. Hence, the "kisses honey"—a hand-rolled cigarette. (Flavier, n.d)

Our idioms are just as difficult and just as confusing for the person new to this country. Yet they are accepted as part of everyday speech. They cannot be translated directly, and their meaning is not always easy to explain.

"He's broke."

"Give me a ring."

"My new car was a real steal."

"I'll drop you a line."

An idiom is often one of several ways of saying the same thing in English. Therefore, it is suggested that idioms be taught as a drill such as the following:

"He's broke. He has no money. He's broke."

Provide several sample sentences so that your student can understand the meaning of the expression and become comfortable with it. There are several good books on idioms. Refer to them for helpful ideas. (See Recommended Books at the end of this text).

WHAT SHOULD I DO IF:

1. **My student does not show up for the first meeting?** The student may well be frightened, so arrange another meeting. Be sure the time and place are understood. If your student understands some English, describe yourself ("I'll be wearing a red coat," or "I'll be carrying a briefcase"). This will help your student to recognize you.

2. **My student does not show up regularly?** Be patient up to a point. Realize that many people from other countries have not been accustomed to schedules. Adhering to

a timetable may be a new and difficult experience. In some cultures it is polite to arrive from fifteen minutes to an hour after the time set. After one or two absences without calls, a tutor should check with the sponsoring group, asking for advice and help. This group should be in a position to recommend a resource person whom you might consult.

3. **My student's progress is slower than I anticipated?** As a tutor you have a responsibility to help your student become independent as quickly as possible. Yet, you must be realistic. To set goals too high and to expect endless hours of study when there are home responsibilities and a full-time job may delay independence.

You may be easily discouraged if you measure your student's progress by your own standards. Patience and praise for small successes will do much to encourage a slow student to try harder. If, after a reasonable length of time, you feel little or no progress is being made, consult your Literacy Volunteer adviser, Literacy Volunteer supervisor, or sponsoring group. It may be best to terminate the tutor-student relationship if either of you are truly dissatisfied. There may be problems beyond your help.

4. **My student's progress is much faster than I anticipated. I wonder if he/she really needs me?** Remember, your student has come **asking** for help in conversational English. It is your responsibility to find out where help is needed. Many conversational English students read and write English beautifully. They speak and comprehend English fairly well, but they want someone to build up their self confidence. They need just a little more practice with someone who understands and will encourage them.

This brings up an interesting point. We are teaching conversational English, and as an organization are committed to teaching survival skills to help people become independent. If you have university students that have conversational English problems, you must decide if this is where your program's resources should go. Does the university that admitted that student recognize their responsibility towards her/his education? Will the student be staying in the United States?

People who are planning to stay in the United States have a prior claim on our training and time. The overwhelming majority of LVA programs deal with with students in the two lowest skill levels of speaking and understanding English. This is in keeping with our basic commitment. But we are an organization of diverse people, and there are always exceptions. One simply has to ask for whom the need is greatest and act as the program has allotted resources. It may be you will have to adjust, to adapt the techniques and methods suggested in this book to a more advanced student.

5. **My student has difficulty understanding and accepting American customs, standards, and ways of doing things?** Some adults are satisfied to stay within their cultural community. It may take considerable diplomacy to confirm your student's heritage and also create a bridge to the new community.

Be aware of possible differences between your student's former culture and the new one to which adjustment is being made, and look for opportunities as you patiently help the newcomer to learn the ways of the new community.

6. **My student brings many home problems to the lesson, leaving very little time for study?** Your primary purpose is educational. You want to help your student learn to understand and speak English and to also be able to read and write at a survival level and thus be able to go into class situations. Be a warm and understanding friend, listening when necessary to personal problems without assuming a counseling role. However, you can best help the student with serious problems by recommending specialists or agencies which can provide professional help.

Modeling the Spoken Language

Learning any language is largely a matter of imitation and practice. Your student must hear and understand what is said in a normal tone and at normal speed. That which is said can then be repeated and the conversation has begun in English, though in a controlled way.

A child learning to talk is constantly imitating and practicing. However, the adult who is learning a second language has one difficulty that the child does not have. The child has no inhibitions in practicing, but the adult, fearful of sounding foolish by mispronouncing words, is much more reticent.

Certainly many of us have studied a foreign language at one time or another, but few of us are comfortable while speaking with a native. We may become self-conscious and tongue-tied, though we might be able to read the written language quite well. Under these circumstances a one-to-one situation may succeed where a group session may not. With rapport between student and tutor established, the student will be more likely to try the new sounds and combination of sounds than if required to do so before an entire class.

Because your student must understand English as it is spoken in the United States and Canada, your speech becomes a model to be followed.

Here are a few **do's and don'ts:**

1. **Don't over-articulate.** Words are often distorted (stoer for **store**.)

2. **Don't speak too slowly.** (The woo-man isss waa-lking dow-en the stree-et.)

3. **Don't speak too loudly.** Your student has no hearing problem.(THE WOMAN IS WALKING DOWN THE STREET.)

4. **Be aware of correct intonation.** The meaning could be changed, for example if the voice rises as in a question. (The woman is walking down the **street**?)

5. **Be aware of incorrect stress.** Avoid the use of unnatural emphasis on certain words. (The woman is **walking** down the **street.)**

6. **Above all, be natural.** (The woman is walking down the street). Use phrases and contractions as you normally would.

The major units of meaning in English are in phrases and sentences, not words. Therefore, **use** phrases and sentences as the basis for instruction.

Also, we usually use contractions, not a full pronoun and a verb construction when making statements:

"I'm hungry."

"You're hungry."

"He's hungry."

It is important that the spoken English your student hears is not distorted but represents the language to be heard in normal conversation. Most people your student hears will not over-articulate, except for emphasis, e.g., "I'm *starved!*" or "Watch *out!*" A student who becomes accustomed to over-articulation or to a speaking rate geared to the lowest level, will find it difficult to converse or to understand normal speech.

It is a mistake for the tutor, in an effort to teach "correct" English to avoid the use of contractions, or slang, or idioms, or to try to pronounce each word individually and distinctly. In everyday English, your student is more likely to hear, *I won't, she's going,* and *he'll come back* than to hear *I will not, she is going,* and *he will come back.* Eventually your student needs to know that *I'm* is a contraction of *I am,* but the shorter version will be more immediately useful in speaking.

Unnatural pitch or wording may interfere with communication. Proper intonation and pronunciation will come more or less naturally with oral practice and need not be drilled separately.

The voice of the native English speaker naturally rises slightly at the end of most questions, instead of dropping as it does in a statement.

"Will you go to the library with me?" The rise of the voice provides an important cue that you are seeking an answer. If you slow down your speech and overemphasize stress and intonation the words can become quite distorted.

Much meaning comes from intonation patterns that we learn through listening and not by rules and specific instruction. Therefore, when the student is learning the spoken language, he/she must hear the words, model them independently by speaking them, then listen again to gain the feedback needed for self-correction. Only then should you proceed to writing those words.

Tutors should not only speak in a normal tone and at normal speed, but should use expressions in normal use:

"How're you this morning?" rather than:

"How are you this morning?" But, most important, be natural, knowing we often speak in fragments that are acceptable.

Q: "What's she doing?"

A: "Fixing the car."

In an effort to communicate with newcomers who understand and speak little English, we sometimes use "Tarzan English," that is, we chop our sentences short, in an effort to be understood. A sponsor, trying to be helpful to her Laotian charge, said "You here stay. I take baby. Wait for you car." The sponsor believed that she was making it easier for the charge to understand. If she had said, "You stay here. I'll take the baby to the car and wait for you there," it would have been just as easy to understand if spoken slowly and with proper stress.

Language should be real and pertinent; it should be real in the sense that it is the type of language people actually speak, not textbook English. It should be real in that the language relates to your student's interests. Work with the vocabulary and objects your student knows and is interested in.

Students are encouraged to repeat sentences with the speed, stress, and intonation of the tutor. If you have modeled a sentence or a structure, and if your student has shown recognition of what you have said and has repeated it, you will have facilitated both initial listening and speaking skills.

Student Survival Kit

In order to "survive", in a language sense, it is necessary to understand and be able to speak certain words. Teaching these survival skills should be a part of every lesson. It is strongly recommended that early in your teaching, you check out your student's ability to handle these survival skills so that you know which ones need further development and practice.

As you get ready to tutor your first lesson, prepare a "Student Survival Kit." It will not only help you in your first lesson but will provide lesson topics relevant to your student's needs for portions of many lessons. You could include these items and others depending on your student's needs. The use of each item is explained below.

1. Student's name, address, telephone number,
2. Alphabet — letter names,
3. Neighborhood map, U.S. and world map,
4. Number cards,
5. Price tags,
6. Money — coins and "play" bills,
7. Student sizes,
8. Cardboard clock,
9. Calendar,
10. Menu,
11. Bus schedule.

STUDENT NAME, ADDRESS, AND TELEPHONE NUMBER

Most conversational English students know their names and addresses in English. Stress the importance of keeping a *written* copy of their name, address, and telephone number with them. Often Americans cannot understand the spoken language of a person just learning English because of a strong accent, and hence cannot give proper directions should the newcomer ask for them. Your help in modeling the student's name, address, and telephone number correctly, may help to avoid an embarrassing or frightening experience.

The telephone is considered a necessity by most people in America. However, it is much more difficult to converse on a telephone than to talk directly to a person since you cannot see the face, eyes, or gestures of the speaker. If you have visited another country and speak little of the language of that country, you know what a frustrating experience talking on the telephone can be. How do you dial? What do you say to the operator? For a person who speaks little English, telephoning in the United States and Canada is equally difficult. Many good lessons can be planned around the use of the telephone. It provides an excellent introduction to dialogue, for a telephone conversation is just that — a dialogue between two people. A toy telephone can be used, or you may want to make a cardboard phone dial. You and your student, back to back, can simulate a real telephone conversation, followed by actual telephone conversation at home as reinforcement.

ALPHABET (LETTER NAMES)

When someone cannot understand a name as spoken, the request usually is to, "Spell it." Thus students need to know the names of the letters in English. Even with those languages whose written characters are the same as English, the letter names are often pronounced differently. For example, the "i" in Spanish is pronounced like our "e" and the letter "e" in Spanish is pronounced like our letter "a".

Take some time in each lesson to pronounce the name of each letter, pointing to the letter and having your student repeat it. You might start with the names of the letters in your student's name, writing the letters in manuscript (printing) as you repeat the letter name.

"L-u-p-e R-i-v-e-r-a"

You may find certain letters are confusing because they sound somewhat alike or look somewhat alike:

a and e
i and y
g, c, z and s
b, p, v and f
g and j

Continue with this kind of practice until the student can:
1. Say the name of each letter as you point at random, and
2. Point to the correct letter as you say the letter name.

You might make small cards (3 by 5 cards quartered), putting individual letters on each one (both capital and small letters). Mix them up and make a game by having your student read letter names at random.

MAPS, DIRECTIONS

Many non-English speakers do not dare to venture from their homes. Fear of becoming lost because they cannot communicate is real—so it seems safer to stay indoors. You can help your student feel more comfortable about venturing out alone by working together to make a neighborhood map. It can be done very simply.

First, discuss how the student gets from home to lessons, noting landmarks and street names as they are mentioned. Note the major points of interest or land marks with pictures or stick figures and print the names of major streets on a sketch of the area to be mapped.

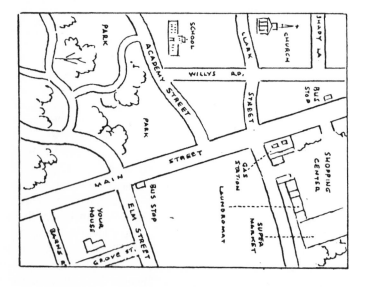

Then, both of you might take a walk, following the map, making any corrections or additions as appropriate. The freedom and confidence a simple, individualized, neighborhood map provides will broaden your student's day-to-day living.

Use the neighborhood map as a visual aid. Start with listening comprehension techniques:

"Point to the school."
"Point to the supermarket."

The next step will be teaching simple questions, asking directions in English:

"Where is the church?"
"Where is the library?"

Continue with practical responses in English:

"It's straight ahead."
"Go left two blocks."
"Go right one block and then left one block."
"Hang a left."
"Turn right at the light."
"You can't miss it."

Maps can also be made for taking public transport. Venturing alone on a bus can be a big undertaking. If it is appropriate, go with your student for the first time, pointing out landmarks.

Make a simple map, showing the number of blocks and where the bus turns. If your student feels inadequate in asking the bus driver for help, write a note to be carried along or teach these instructions:

"Please tell me when the bus gets to Main and Elm streets."

NUMBERS AND MONEY

Will Durant in **Our Oriental Heritage** (1954, p.79) writes that "Counting was probably one of the earliest forms of speech and in many tribes it still presents a relieving simplicity. The Tasmanians counted up to two: 'Parmery, calabawa, cardia, i.e. 'one, two, plenty'; the Guaranis of Brazil adventured further and said: 'One, two, three, four, innumerable'…Counting was by the fingers, hence the decimal system. When — apparently after some time — the idea of twelve was reached, the number became a favorite because it was pleasantly divisible by five of the first six digits; and that duo-decimal system was born which obstinately survives in English measurement today: twelve months in a year, twelve pence in a shilling, twelve units in a dozen, twelve dozen in a gross, twelve inches in a foot. Thirteen, on the other hand, refused to be divided, and became disreputable and unlucky forever."

The following discussion of numbers and money is adapted from material presented at TESOL Conference Los Angeles, CA, 1975

Numbers are important in everyday life. Think how often they're needed:

telephone numbers,
house numbers,
prices,
weights and sizes.

Numbers must be *exact*. Mispronunciation of a word, or poor grammar can be tolerated, but a wrong number isn't permitted. When discussing prices, even knowing where to put the word *dollars* is important. *Two hundred fifty dollars* is very different from *two dollars and fifty cents.*

How would you say these numbers?

1776 — You probably said, Seventeen Seventy-six because you assume it's a date, but it could be *one seven, six.*

437-8381 — *Four three seven eight three eight one* because you assume it's a telephone number. But it could be *four hundred thirty-seven dash eight thousand three hundred eighty-one.*

$3.50 — *Three dollars and fifty cents* or *three fifty* or *three and a half.* All mean the same thing.

1249 — *Twelve forty-nine* or *one thousand two hundred forty nine.*

6.2 — *Six point two* or *six and two tenths.*

1/10 — *One tenth*

Imagine how confusing it must be to a student to learn that we say the same number in many ways. Your student must not only be able to "say" the numbers, knowing which numbers are meant (*seventy nine* is 79 and *ninety seven* is 97), but the student must also recognize them when someone speaks them. If *seventeen nine (179)* is heard when you say *seventy-nine (79),* there will probably be many problems when shopping.

Numbers are among the first items to be taught. First, give your student a list of the first ten numbers, pointing to each number as you give the name. Point to 1 and say "one." Have your student repeat the name twice. Then, on to 2, 3...10. At the end of ten numbers, review. When you're sure your student knows the names of these numbers, point to them at random, asking for the names of the numbers. This is a bit more difficult, and you may find your student counting silently (1-2-3-4-5-6-) to get *seven.*

Then increase the difficulty. Say a number and have the student point to it. Usually, it's much more difficult to "hear" and identify a number than to recognize the number and say its name.

Reverse the roles. Have the student say a number and you point to it. Sometimes one number will be called for, but another will be intended. Perhaps the student will say *eighteen* (18) and mean *eighty* (80). This will make quite a difference if it refers to a price or an address!

Continue through the teens. Then — 20, 30, 40, 50, will come easier. Teach the different ways of saying prices, $2.98 is *two dollars and ninety eight cents,* or *two ninety eight,* for short. Reverse the process and have the student give you prices. Write down the figure that your student dictates. Was that what was intended?

At an other lesson, you could pretend you're a store clerk. Have your student ask the price of something and you give the price. Have the student listen, and write down the numbers heard. When you said, *"Nineteen ninety",* your student may have heard $90.90.

Each teaching session could include five to ten minutes on numbers. Review and repetition give the confidence needed.

Continue with more advanced work in numbers by supplying information and requesting an answer.

"How many windows are there in the room?"

"How many days are in a year?"

"How many pages are in this book?"

"Turn to page 362."

If a student can add, divide, and multiply in his own language, provide simple mathematical problems.

"Please add this column of figures:"

```
  74
  26
  19
____
```

"Multiply these numbers:"

```
 427
  42
____
```

The student is learning to "think" the numbers in English, too.

Most countries use the metric system and the USA is gradually changing over to this system. But until the metric system is universal, your student will have to know our present system of measurements, too: an inch, a foot, a yard, his or her clothing sizes. One way to help your student when shopping would be to prepare a written list of his/her sizes as known in the United States, e.g.:

suit — size 36 regular,
shirt — 15-32,
underwear — 34-36 (medium),
socks — size 12,
shoes — size 10B,
dress — Size 16,
stockings — size 10,
slip — size 38,
shoes — size 7B,
underwear — size 6.

It's also important for the student to know his/her height in feet and inches and weight in pounds. You can make a short lesson out of this information by bringing a tape measure and/or scales and explaining their use to the student. At this point you might insert some cultural information that Americans mignt tell you how tall they are but will seldom talk about their weight. Women are often sensitive about telling their age.

TIMES AND DATES

Americans are usually very punctual. Our activities are governed by the clock. If a bus is scheduled to leave at 10:42, it doesn't mean "about" that time. If you have a dental appointment at 9:30 a.m., you'd better be there a few minutes early. Because this idea of time and punctuality is not universal, you will need to discuss American's ideas about time, both public and social, and teach your student to tell time. You can use a real clock or make one out of cardboard. Start with the hours.

1:00 — *one o'clock*
2:00 — *two o'clock*

Then,
1:30 — *one thirty*
2:30 — *two thirty*

Follow this by:

1:15 — *one fifteen, or fifteen after one, or quarter past one.* Be consistent by using only one form at the beginning, giving alternates later.

Take your cue from your student if he speaks some English. For example, if he says *quarter to two,* reinforce that before giving alternates.

Digital clocks are commonly used in America. It is sometimes easier to read time from a digital clock, i.e.

1:15 — one-fifteen

4:40 — four-forty

Realize, too, that as much as we Americans go rigidly "by the clock", there are other times when special information is needed.

Air flight time of 1:30 p.m. means you should arrive at the airport at least one half hour early for boarding, because the plane actually leaves the ground at 1:30 p.m.

A clinic appointment at 2:30 p.m. means you should arrive a few minutes early.

A job — 9.a.m. to 5 p.m. — means exactly that. Be ready to start at nine and work until five.

An invitation to a reception or a cocktail party from "6-8" means you arrive sometime after six and leave at any time before eight. Guests are not expected to arrive before the stated time.

Students should also learn to use a calendar if they do not already know how to do so. In fact, a calendar is a useful device for teaching and practicing English.

Pronounce the months of the year and the days of the week as you point to them on the calendar. You might want to provide your student with a calendar, writing down the days of your lessons, as well as other important information.

Your student may or may not be able to say the names of the months or the days of the week. Model them and have the student repeat. But also be sure your student can *hear* and *understand* them. You could say "Tuesday", and ask the student to point on the calendar to the appropriate column.

One student couldn't understand why his fellow workers laughed when he said he'd be back on *thirsty.* He said, with a question in his eyes, "Sunday, Monday, Tuesday, Wednesday, Thirsty?" Gently the tutor explained the difference between *thirsty* and *Thursday.* But they do sound very much alike, don't they?

You are now ready to move on to that first lesson.

CHAPTER 7
The First Session

What to Bring...What to Say...What to Do (Gestures, Colored Paper Drill)
What to Bring

As you go into your lessons there are certain materials that you should have with you. These materials should prove helpful when you feel the need for a change of pace in an actual lesson. It can help you survive a rough place in the lesson, and it also provides survival information for your student.

If your student has not been tested before being assigned to you, you won't know if your student can speak English at all, or if their language skills will be at level I, II, III, or IV, so you will not be able to have a real lesson plan ready for the first session.

However, you can bring your "bag of tricks" with you and give your student appropriate tasks geared to his/her level of ability at the very first lesson. Bring:

1. **Information about your student:** name, address, phone number, country, etc.
2. **ESLOA.** (Giving this as part of the first session should tell you quickly the speaking and comprehension level of the student.)
3. **Notebook and pen.**
4. **Objects for simple drill:** book, comb, purse, etc.
5. **Colored Paper Strips** to teach listening comprehension skills to beginning level students.
6. **Bilingual dictionary** (English and the language of your student)
7. **Student Survival Kit:** (Discussed fully in Chapter 6)
   Student's name, address, and telephone number,
   Alphabet — letter cards,
   Number cards,
   Price tags,
   Money — coins and play bills,
   Neighborhood map, U.S. and world maps,
   Student sizes,
   Cardboard clock,
   Calendar and watch (to make your next date),
   Menu,
   Bus schedules,
   Stick figure cards, photos of your family,
8. **National Geographic** (or any other magazine) that has pictures, an article, or a map of your student's country.
9. Your name, address, telephone number written out to leave with your student.

What to Say

The first session with your student is most important, as you are setting the climate for future meetings. Don't let your desire to be friendly make you too effusive.

Speaking distinctly, introduce yourself, saying simply, "Hello, my name is _____." If your student responds with "Hello" and gives his or her name, that's fine. If your student merely smiles when you ask "What's your name?" you know the student probably doesn't under-stand one word of English and cannot even respond with his/her name. Start right there.

Point to your student and say (his or her name). Point to yourself and say "John Doe" — or whatever your name is. Repeat this procedure to make sure your student understands it. Then point to yourself and say, "My name is _____." Repeat this several times as clearly as you can. Then point to your student, inserting your student's name, "My name is _____" gesturing for him or her to repeat. (You say "my" when saying your student's name, for your student will repeat your exact words.) In practice, this procedure is not confusing, and an average student will catch on quickly.

However, if a student can answer all the questions in Levels I and II in the ESLOA test (see Chapter 4), it would be foolish to work long on simple introductions. You'd want to start at a more advanced level. Take your cue from your student. Even if your student answers some of the questions, remember that the knowledge of English is probably limited or your help would not have been solicited.

Your first session will be a "get acquainted" session and a time to begin to learn what the language needs of your student are. Your student will be looking you over, wondering how it will all work out. You will be assessing your student's abilities — strengths and weaknesses — and striving to build up the confidence you both need. As you make plans for your next meeting, be sure to write down the date and time. If your student cannot read this, surely a friend or family member can help.

A friendly "Hello" and "Good-by" in English can begin and end each session, but you might want to learn "Hello" and "Good-by" in your student's language. You would have a taste of a new language and would certainly put your student at ease, sharing a pride in that language, too.

What to Do

GESTURES

One of the first things you will want to do is to establish some useful gestures needed for nonverbal communication with your student. The following have proven successful with various students.

1. **Listen.** You can indicate to your student that you want no speaking, only listening by cupping your hand next to your ear, perhaps putting a finger on your lips and saying, "Listen" or "Shh".

2. **Repeat** When you want your student to repeat what you say, point to the student, using the charade gesture meaning "Come on," (hand open, palm up, fingers pointing toward yourself.)

3. **Respond** If you want your student to respond or answer a question, open your hand, palm up, toward your student.

4. **Tutor responds** When you expect to respond yourself, point to yourself as you start talking.

5. **Speak together** When you want your student to say something with you, point one hand at yourself and gesture with the other hand toward your student, as in charades.

Whichever gestures you decide are comfortable for you to use, make sure you use the same ones consistently. Also try to find out if they may carry some negative nonverbal signal in your student's culture.

Be aware that some American gestures and body movement may be offensive to people of other cultures.

To many newcomers the following are offensive (McMichael, Coor) —
    hands on hips,
    slouching,
    sitting on a desk,
    yawning,
    stretching,
    counting people with index finger and wide arm movement,
    beckoning with index finger or pointing to person with a left hand,
    giving anything with the left hand.

To East Asians, these actions are not acceptable:
    touching student of the opposite sex,
    touching a person on the head,
    hugging,
    passing something over someone's head.

To Arabs, these actions are offensive:
    touching or hugging a person of the opposite sex,
    showing someone the sole of your foot,
    giving something (especially food) with the left hand,
    turning your back on someone during conversation,
    winking.

To Latins, the "OK" sign so often used by Americans, is offensive.

Just knowing some of these may help you become sensitive to your student's outlook as you work together.

USING COLORED PAPER

Listening and understanding are going to be the first skills that you will teach the completely non-English speaking student. Using commands which require a physical response is a very good way to introduce new sentence structures and vocabulary to the beginning student. A very practical and easy way to do this is by using slips of colored paper. (Adapted from Gattegno, 1972)

From the very first lesson your student will hear complete English sentences and can react to them in such a way as to demonstrate an understanding of what is heard. You will be teaching simple sentences and you can add new vocabulary as quickly or as slowly as is necessary for your student.

Materials Required:

Slips of colored paper (blue, red, yellow, etc.), sizes 1″ x 6″, 1″ x 5″, 1″ x 3″ for each color.

The vocabulary used will be controlled and limited to the following words in portions of specific lessons:

Lesson 1. *the, paper, blue, red, I, pick, up, put, on, table, a;*

Lesson 2. *give, me, point, to, black, yellow, take;*

Lesson 3. *touch, it, him, her, one, two, three;*

Lesson 4. *white, green, down;*

Lesson 5. *on, under, between,* (more colors);

Lesson 6. *big, bigger, biggest, small, smaller, smallest;*

Lesson 7. *Next, to, here, there;*

Lesson 8. *right, left, hand, quickly, slowly;*

Lesson 9. other useful words.

For the first lesson, use three blue and three red slips of paper. The new vocabulary will include only basic words that go along with your actions.

Your student doesn't see these words in writing but hears them as you say them when you demonstrate with the pieces of paper. At first your student may try to repeat what you say. Discourage this by gesturing that the student should listen only.

Pick up any slip of paper and say, "a paper," at a normal speed. Repeat this with each piece of paper. Repetition gives confidence in understanding what you have said.

Then pick up a blue piece of paper (any size) and say, "a blue paper," repeating for each blue piece of paper. Repeat this action with a piece of red paper.

Pick up a blue piece of paper and say, "I pick up a blue paper." Put it down and say, "I put the blue paper on the table." Repeat this to be sure your student understands. And repeat it with the red paper.

When you feel that your student understands what you have said as you demonstrated, push the six pieces of paper to the student's side of the table and tell the student, "Pick up a paper." If your student doesn't understand, you can help by motioning to the student to take the paper, or even taking his/her hand and helping. Be sensitive to the fact that in some cultures, touching is resented.

Then reach out to receive the paper and say, "Give me a paper." If there is no understanding, take the paper and continue:
    "Pick up a blue paper."
    "Give me a blue paper."
    "Pick up a red paper."
    "Give me a red paper."

Continue manipulating these patterns until you are sure your student understands all the words. Your student may be concentrating so hard on following directions that the colors become confusing. Be patient. Go only as fast as is comfortable. Reassure the student with verbal praise and a warm smile.

This is an excellent ice-breaker for a student who can speak no English at all. Confidence can be built up quickly because of active response rather than passive listening.

But what about the advanced student? You can use colored paper exercises with *any* level student.

The following commands can be quite complicated:

"Pick up three green papers and put down two red papers."

"Put two blue papers in the box, giving me four red papers, keeping one red paper yourself."

"Hold all the red papers in your left hand, but pick up two yellow papers with your right hand, giving them to me."

You can teach the concept of the size (larger or smaller), position (on, under, next to) or distance (two steps, across the room), as listening skills, using colored paper when appropriate.

"Put the largest black paper between the smallest red and green papers."

"Put the smallest green paper in the blue book across the room, between pages 311 and 312."

"Take the smaller of the two red papers on your left, and put it on top of the larger green paper on your right."

You might like to vary the exercise by using red, blue and yellow pencils or books with different colored bindings after you are sure your student understands the vocabulary and sentence structure you have been practicing.

Much work and practice will be needed on listening skills. Use a variety of materials so that practice doesn't become boring to your student. Direction and new words are presented orally, not in written form, as you practice listening skills. Your notes or lesson plans are, of course, written, but these are for **your use** only.

That first session can lead to a meaningful experience for both of you, as you learn more about each other and develop skills in verbal communication.

CHAPTER 8
Techniques for Levels I - IV

Sentence Structure...Listening and Understanding...Comprehension Checks... Basic Oral Drills...Dialogues...Creative Drills

In this chapter, our attention will be focused on teaching listening-speaking skills. Since language is a system, learners must be shown *through example* what the system is. Learning the basic patterns or structure of the language, (i.e. the forms and arrangements of words) is primary. Acquisition of vocabulary is a secondary but vital goal. Therefore, the techniques presented in this book will suggest ways for teaching both structure and vocabulary, which together convey the message of the speaker or the author.

The methods should remain flexible. They are yours to adapt...combine...modify...enjoy! Learning a new language can be a difficult process but it doesn't have to be dreary as well. If you find teaching your student a happy challenge, this attitude will be contagious.

Sentence Structure

When thinking of the structure of the English language, most of us do not analyze *why* we say something in a certain way. We say it the way we do because it sounds right. For example, we wouldn't say,

"I to work go." but rather,

"I go to work."

We couldn't say,

"This pencil not is sharp." or,

"This pencil not sharp is."

We'd say,

"This pencil is not sharp."

Perhaps we can't always tell what grammatical rules are being followed when we speak "standard English" but as long as we speak it, does it really matter? Your aim as a tutor will be to teach the standard usage so that your student will get the feel for the accepted form of spoken English.

Grammatically correct sentences will then sound right to your student and confusing rules about language and grammar can be avoided. Often, you as a tutor, will want to know *why* something is said in a certain way, but avoid talking about the rules of grammar to your student. Instead, teach correct usage by practicing with properly structured phrases and sentences. This does not mean that you should not answer any questions about grammar from your student, however, only that you should avoid lengthy discussions.

Many of the techniques that we have already discussed help to build the student's sense of what sounds right in English. Dialogues, drills and games all reinforce the student's developing feel for English sentence structure.

In teaching sentence structure, you must be aware that proper word order is essential for accurate communication

and that the same words can convey a totally different meaning when their order in a sentence is changed. For example, every speaker of English knows that although identical vocabulary is used in these two sentences, they describe two totally different experiences:

"The dog bit the man."

"The man bit the dog."

Word order is therefore an essential element of accurate communication. You will teach English word order by having your student associate word order with meanings and having him produce words in their correct order himself.

If you are working with a beginning student, use sentences you can illustrate.

"The book is on the table."

"The book is on the chair."

"The book is on the floor."

Especially for beginning students it is suggested that you limit the introduction of structures to one new structure in any individual lesson, working on that until it is mastered. Because your student will be repeating your sentence, the grammar will be correct.

At times you may want to prepare simple grammar checks for the student. Two kinds are possible:

1. "Right or wrong?"
2. "Which one is it?

In "right or wrong", you say a sentence in English. Once in a while, say a sentence which has the wrong word order or grammar, such as:

T — "She live in Smallville."

S — Wrong.

If you have already practiced this grammar structure, the student should recognize this sentence as wrong. Then immediately, follow the wrong sentence with the right one.

T — "She lives in Smallville."

S — "Right."

Which one is it? is another listening (or reading) check of grammar. For a simple grammar contrast (singular or plural; male or female; "now"or "everyday"), prepare 6-10 sentences. Say them and have the student indicate which grammar concept is being used.

T — "He's swimming." (now)

T — "He eats at Big Burger." (every day)

T — "She cooks dinner." (every day)

T — "She's drinking a Coke." (now)

T — "They're riding the bus." (now)

T — "They work at the factory." (every day)

These grammar checks help to build the student's sense of what sounds right, yet you can avoid confusing grammar explanations. (Based on Donna Ilyin's reference: mini check ideas published in several books by Alemany Press.)

Listening and Understanding

When visiting the Soviet Union and Turkey I found not knowing the spoken language was not only most frustrating but also limiting as to what I could do and where I could go. Even if I had memorized the words to ask a question, it would have been impossible for me to understand the answer. Non-English speakers in America are similarly limited because they cannot understand our spoken language.

Listening and understanding are the first skills a student must learn, and this can be accomplished before the person can speak a word of the new language.

The emphasis at the beginning, perhaps for several lessons, should be on listening comprehension, with your student responding to actions, or other "language-easy" ways. This can be done by a physical response from your student — no oral response in English or in the native language is necessary. The responses are in the actions of the student. By appropriate performance, you can know if there is understanding. This is a very important part of your teaching.

COMMANDS

For a beginning conversational English student, start simply. At first use simple commands which direct the student to action, demonstrating as you speak. "Stand up." Repeat the command and stand up again. When you think the student's ears are accustomed to both the sounds of the English command, and its meaning, then gesture to your student to stand up. "Sit down." Again, demonstrate and give time for it to be understood, and suggest the desired response. Then, "Walk." "Stop", and "Turn around." The tutor walks, stops and turns around to demonstrate.

Then perhaps you can go on to such commands as "Point to…" and "Touch…". Combine these directions with *door, table, window, floor,* or designate parts of the body to identify, such as *nose, fingers, head, and ears.* A simple command could be, "Point to the door," or "Point to your head." Continue with such commands as "Close…", "Pick up…", and combine these with *book, pen, door, window,* or anything else available.

Use one structure at a time, changing only one word.
"Point to the book."
"Point to the table."

Varying the structure and the new vocabulary at the same time would be confusing to the beginning student. Use a variety of commands only if your student is more advanced.
"Point to the table."
"Pick up the yellow pencil."

COMMANDS Directing Your Student to Action		
Stand up. Sit down. Walk.		Turn around. Stop.
Point to	the door. the table. the window.	the floor. the book. the pen.

Touch	your nose. your finger. your hand. your head.
Pick up	the book. the red book. the black book. the green book.

Add others, such as *give, take, open, close* as you work with your student.

Questions

Another simple way to teach listening and understanding is by the use of questions. Some questions are easier to answer than others. The easiest are the "yes-no" questions. Then the "either-or" ones.

If you ask the question, "Is this pencil red or black" you've supplied the answer and yet your student had to understand the question to choose the correct response.

Much work and practice will be needed on listening skills. Directions and new words are presented orally, not in written form, as you practice listening skills. Your notes or lesson plans are, of course, written, but these are for **your use** only.

MORE ON LISTENING SKILLS

Words which have different meanings from one culture to another often make misunderstandings possible, sometimes with serious results.

A major concern to the police in a large city is loitering. Puerto Rican newcomers often do not know of laws against this on the mainland of the United States, since there is no such law in Puerto Rico. In Puerto Rico, they are accustomed to meeting in small, friendly groups in the street. When they do so in a city on the mainland, they may be asked politely to go home, and they usually oblige. However, if they persist in staying, a police officer may tell them they will be arrested for loitering if they don't disperse. The Puerto Ricans use a word similar to the English word loitering (loteria) but it means the numbers game! This confusion may compound the problem for both the parties involved without their knowing why. (Senior, 1965)

Some students can read and write English well, but they need special help in the listening skills. Have the student listen as you read aloud and respond in an informal way as you ask questions and solicit information-stimulated discussions.

Telephone conversations call for listening skills. There are no gestures, no eyes to help communication. The ears alone must do the work. Occasional telephone calls give excellent training. There is a special need for enunciating clearly on the phone. One of the Spanish-speaking students kept hearing *all of you* as *I love you*. You can imagine the complications this might evoke.

Students who read in their own language may resist practising listening skills because they are attuned to written messages. Such students may not be able to understand a conversation or a radio broadcast in English. They know more at "eye level" that at "ear level" and often insist on seeing the word in print. This may defeat the very purpose of their work with you. Encourage them to *listen* for comprehension of a word, phrase, or sentence. To rely on *seeing* the word first enables them to translate it into their native language and allows them to completely skip the oral language they are attempting to acquire.

One way to deal with this need for the printed word is to provide the student with word cards at the end of the lesson to be used for rehearsal of vocabulary between sessions. For people who "see" words in their minds, this is another way of imprinting the ENGLISH word in their memory.

You could suggest that a lecture or broadcast be recorded and then it could be listened to again and again, as aften as necessary. You could suggest that both you and your student listen to the same radio or TV news broadcast and discuss it at a lesson together. By giving your student an opportunity to review what was heard, you have helped develop the thinking skills needed for effective listening now and effective reading later.

Comprehension Checks

Some people will speak and read words in English which they do not understand. Be careful not to assume comprehension simply because the words were pronounced correctly.

During a tutoring session, you can often sense that your student doesn't understand a word you have said — sometimes by a quizzical look, a cocking of the head, or raised eyebrows.

If you ask "Do you understand?", new students will often smile and say "yes." They're embarrassed that they don't understand. Too, they think they're pleasing *you* by saying they understand. If you have a bilingual dictionary available, look up the word. If your student reads in his own language, show him the comparable word in his language. A smile of comprehension shows that the problem has been resolved.

Pictures, actions, and basic question patterns can help ascertain whether or not your student really understands the meaning of both the spoken and written language.

Sometimes certain words will confuse your student because they sound alike to him:

vest	best
moon	noon
soup	soap
letter	ladder

This is how you might identify the differences between the words *letter* and *ladder*. Repeat the word *letter* as you point to a letter of the alphabet or a piece of correspondence, asking your student to repeat the word *letter*. Say the word "ladder" as you point to a picture of a ladder. Put the words in sentences, asking the student to repeat:

"I wrote a letter to my friend."
"He climbed the ladder to fix the roof."

Students get practice both from hearing and saying the sounds in contrast and also from associating each word with an object that might help him fix it in his mind. You know

your student has differentiated between the two words when both words are used correctly in a sentence.

It should be obvious that an important part of your job in teaching language skills to an conversational English student is to assure comprehension of what you say If you ask, "Do you understand?" a nod or even a response of, "Yes," does not guarantee comprehension. It is therefore necessary to find other ways to determine the degree of understanding. One way is to have student action follow a direction.

"Pick up the pencil."

If the student picks up the pencil, there is understanding.

"Open the window and tell me what you did."
If your student not only opens the window but says:
"I opened the window."
you know there is both understanding and ability to respond in English. If the response is:
"I open…"
you model the correct response:
"I opened the window."
gesturing for the student to repeat the entire sentence.

How you state a question often determines what kind of response you get. There are questions where a "Yes" or "No"response is appropriate.

"Is the door closed?"
"Is the book blue?"

Although the "Yes" or "No" questions are "language easy", the student must understand the whole question in order to answer correctly.

Other questions can be phrased to allow for alternate answers.

"Is the door open or closed?"
"Is the book red or blue?"

With these questions, the right answer is contained in the question. In a way, your "either-or" questions are both teaching *and* checking comprehension at the same time.

Still other questions demand more language in the answer — the *wh* questions (who, which, where, what and when) and the *how* questions require that the student state a fact.

"Who is President of the United States?"

"When was the Constitution of the United States written?"
"Where is Toronto?"
Some questions require descriptive answers.
"How is corn grown?"
Phrasing a question another way invites a comparative statement.
"What is the difference between the climate in your country and the climate here?"
Advanced students can be asked more problem questions, demanding greater knowledge and requiring more inference:
"If you were to go to the moon, what would you expect to find?"
The tutor varies the level of difficulty of the questions in accordance with the ability of the individual student.
In addition to asking questions, the following technique will be useful in determining the student's command of listening comprehension.
The tutor and the student sit back to back. The tutor gives an instruction, such as:
"Put the pencil on the left side of the book."
"Put the cup on top of the book."
Both the tutor and the student follow the instructions. Then both turn around to compare what they have done. It's fun to do the same things together, and it presents a good check on simple comprehension.

Comprehension Checks

1. Action to follow directions.
2. Questions.
3. Back-to-back session with common directions.

Basic Oral Drills

Early in my experimentation with teaching conversational English, I decided that it might be practical to have a two-way program: each participant of the team of two having an opportunity to be student and tutor. I would be the main tutor to someone who wanted to learn to speak English, and I would teach during our first hour together. My student, who spoke only Spanish, might want to teach me to speak Spanish in our second hour together.

Our one rule was that in the first hour, only English could be spoken, while in the second hour, only Spanish could be spoken. I had had some training in basic drills and techniques and tried to explain to Francisca, my Spanish speaking student, that she would model her lessons in Spanish on my lessons in English.

We certainly enjoyed the lessons and became good friends, laughing at our mistakes and rejoicing in our successes. We soon found out, to my dismay, that Francesca was progressing faster in English than I was in Spanish. Her pronunciation was better and her memory, longer. Her progress did much for her morale and she tried to praise and encourage me.

I am sure much of Francesca's success and my failure was due to the fact that she was a faster learner than I was. But I tried to be realistic. Living in a community where English is spoken all around you helps give one a "feel" for the language. My student got this "feel" but I heard no Spanish except at the few hour lessons I had each week. Learning a new language is much easier when one is living in a setting where that language is spoken. Even a beginner can occasionally hear some words which are recognized. At the very least, there is an opportunity to practice such simple words as *yes, no, hello,* and *goodbye.*

I realized more than ever how important it was to use established techniques — and how important repetition was. I used substitution drills early in our lessons, using objects in our teaching room:
"It's a book."
"It's a chair."
"It's a desk."
"It's a window."
I repeated and repeated until Francesca had the pattern and the vocabulary. Then the questions:
"What's this?"
"It's a book."
"What's this?"
"It's a chair."
I was pleased with her progress and she had gained confidence. But what was happening during the second half of the lesson when I was supposedly learning Spanish? I had lost most of my confidence. Even though I studied diligently at home, I found I had trouble remembering the vocabulary and had to resort to Spanish books. I wasn't speaking naturally and I was *translating* according to written words I tried to remember.

My Spanish tutor tried to use the substitution drill with me, but she had no training. She didn't fully understand the technique of changing only *one* word within the pattern each time. Our lessons in Spanish would go something like this (except in Spanish, of course):
"This is a book."
"That, over there, is a chair."
"Here is a desk."
"That's a window."
I'd repeat each sentence (I'm a good mimic), and Francesca was delighted. Because I had repeated the statement, my tutor thought I knew it. I felt the need for repetition and tried to repeat the statements, but my tutor was so pleased with me that she wanted me to go on. Because the second sentence, telling me it was "a chair" was not exactly in the same pattern, I had trouble knowing which word was *chair* and I couldn't possibly remember each entire sentence. When my Spanish teacher went back to ask, "What is this?" pointing to a book, my mind was a complete blank. Needless to say, the experience was frustrating to both of us. That's when we decided to concentrate only on English. I'd have to learn my Spanish later or elsewhere.

So, there is a real need to know and practice these simple but effective drills. They are designed to help in teaching the speaking skills, which closely follow the listening skills.

In teaching English, you should always use sentences, rather than isolated words, speaking as you normally would. Americans often use contractions and the student must understand and use them. You wouldn't say:
"Here is a book"
"It is a book"
You would say,

"Here's a book."
"It's a book."

Using such expressions, as your student will hear them in normal circumstances, will be a preparation for the understanding of spoken English when you are not around.

SUBSTITUTION DRILL

The substitution drill is really quite simple. You merely substitute one word for another in the same sentence. Be sure your student understands what you say. Start with sentences about objects in the room, or pictures, or use action verbs that can be demonstrated. Pointing to an object, you could say (gesturing for the student to repeat).

"It's a chair."
"It's a pencil."
"It's a book."

You do this drill so that your student gets intensive practice with a single grammatical structure. Don't be misled into thinking your student can say these sentences independently just because they are repeated easily. Repeat this same sentence several times. Repetition builds confidence and assures later success.

You can reinforce the student's pronunciation by repeating after the student:

T — "It's a book."
S — "It's a book."
T — "It's a book."
T — "It's a pencil."
S — "It's a pencil."
T — "It's a pencil. "

A word of caution when using the substitution drill! As you substitute a new word in a sentence, there is a tendency to overemphasize that word. Your student, using you as a model, will do the same thing. You might be using pictures to demonstrate:

"The *man's* running."
"The *woman's* running."

In a normal conversation you probably wouldn't stress *man* or *woman* unless you were comparing the man and the woman. You might even stress the word *running* if you had been talking about a disability. Therefore, generally, as you substitute words in a structure, be careful to talk with natural stress and intonation.

"The man's running."
"The woman's running."

If you are using action verbs, be sure the action corresponds to the sentence. Be sure both you and your student are seated as you say, "I'm sitting." Stand up and gesture for the student to stand, as you say "I'm standing." Start walking, and encourage the student to walk, as you say,"I'm walking."

Once the student has learned even a simple speech pattern, show how it can be used again and again by simply substituting just one word.

I'm	eating. reading. carrying.	

You're They're	carrying	the book. the books.
He's She's I'm We're	reading eating	a newspaper. a recipe. my lunch. our dinner.

You can make this simple substitution drill more challenging by changing two words instead of one, keeping the structure the same:

"It's a green pencil."
"It's a red book."

This same substitution drill can be used for a more advanced student by first giving the structure:

"The family is going to the clinic." (Show an appropriate picture.)

Then give only the word to be substituted, e.g. *supermarket, library, school*. The drill will go like this:

T — "The family is going to the clinic."
S — "The family is going to the clinic."
T — "...supermarket."
S — "The family is going to the supermarket."
T — "...library."
S — "The family is going to the library."
T — "...school."
S — "The family is going to the school."

The substitution drill is a "simple drill" when the same slot is substituted. The "slot" may consist of one or more words. The drill is much more difficult and called a "complex drill" when the word or words supplied have to go in different slots in the sentence. He has to think about the meaning of the word and know whether the word fits a subject slot, or a verb slot.

You can add to the complexity by varying the word you give for substitution. The student must be very alert because he will never know where the next substitution will be.

T — "The family is going to the clinic."
S — "The family is going to the clinic."
T — "...girl."
S — "The girl is going to the clinic."
T — "...walking."
S — "The girl is walking to the clinic."
T — "...bus."
S — "The girl is walking to the bus."

Substitution Drill
Simple

Substitute one word in a sentence, with an appropriate action for comprehension.

"Here's a book."
"Here's a chair."
"Here's my pencil."
"I'm sitting."
"You're sitting."
"We're sitting."

RESPONSE DRILL

An early step toward getting your student to be independent is to work on *response drills*. Through the previous substitution drill, you have already taught the student the answers needed to certain questions. Through repetition, the student will begin to sense a pattern of the answers. Now you can ask the student to *use* what has been practiced.

For the beginning student, actions and pictures must supplement the drill. And, of course you must be certain before you ask the question that your student has the information and language practice needed for the answer. You are not quizzing for facts! You are giving repeated practice in understanding and responding to common questions. Thus, your procedure should always be to model and teach the answer first, having the student repeat, and then ask the question.

    T — "I'm walking around the table."
    S — "I'm walking around the table."
    T — "What are you doing?"
    S — "I'm walking around the table."

Eventually you will reverse the positions. Have the student ask the question and you answer.

    S — "What are you doing?"
    T — "I'm walking around the table."

Be careful not to ask questions beyond your student's comprehension. Keep to questions whose answers were practiced in the lesson's substitution drill. Build on words already known and help your student learn to say words or sentences used in ordinary conversation.

For example, you can teach, "I'm studying English". When your student can say that with fairly good pronunciation and normal intonation, and you are sure it is understood, ask the question, "What are you studying?" Then practice the reverse as the student asks the question and you give the answer.

When you have taught a basic structure such as:
"I'm going to the library,"
you can vary it easily. The question would be:
"Where are you going?"
You could stimulate various responses by showing different pictures:
"I'm going to the library."
"I'm going to the post office."
"I'm going to the supermarket."
Response drill could include a pretend visit to the grocery store to shop for food and teach the student the various ways we sell it — by the pound, by the loaf, by the dozen.

    T — "I'll have a dozen rolls."
    S — "I'll have a dozen rolls."
    T — "I'll have a loaf of bread."
    S — "I'll have a loaf of bread."
    T — "I'll have a pound of cheese."
    S — "I'll have a pound of cheese."
Then the questions:
    T — "What would you like?"
    S — "I'll have a dozen rolls."
    T — "What would you like?"
    S — "I'll have a loaf of bread."
    T — "What would you like?"
    S — "I'll have a pound of cheese."

Notice that what you are doing is actually combining Response Drill with a Substitution Drill.

Another time the two of you can actually act out a response drill. Be sure the action corresponds to the sentence.

    T — "I'm sitting at the table."
    S — "I'm sitting at the table."
    T — "What are you doing?"
    S — "I'm sitting at the table."

Early in the teaching sequence you may want to help a homemaker student become familiar with the names of various types of appliances or pieces of furniture in her home. You can use stick pictures or actual pictures, as you use the response drill.

As your student advances, use pictures to elicit a variety of responses. You won't have to model the response. It will come naturally, depending on the picture, the vocabulary, and the student's experience.

    T — "What's this man doing?"
    S — "He's fishing."
    T — "What's this man doing?"
    S — "He's walking."
    T — "What's this man doing?"
    S — "He's running."

Questions about pictures often give your student a chance to provide a wide range of answers. As you ask the question, "What's the girl doing?" you might expect the answer, "The girl's sitting," but your student might say, "The girl's smiling", or "The girl's playing." The student is able to use the acquired vocabulary independently. That's growth.

Creating their own questions is the goal for students. They'll need to learn to ask questions *they'll* need the answers to. They'll need to understand a practical response, too.

    S — "Where do I get the bus for Main Street?"
    T — "Go to the next corner. It comes every ten minutes."

Using Response Drills will help your student begin to use the English they need for real-life communication.

TRANSFORMATION DRILLS

In the transformation drill, the student

1. Changes positive statements into negative statements, and conversely, negative statements into positive statements.

2. Changes statements to questions and questions to statements.

3. Changes present tense sentences to past tense sentences, (or other). As with other drills, the student works on only one change at a time.

Prepare the student for changing a positive statement into a negative one by having both the positive and the negative sentences repeated after you. Pictures or quickly drawn stick figures insure comprehension.

T — "The man is happy."
S — "The man is happy."

Shake your head as you say,

T — "The man is not happy"
S — "The man is not happy."

After the student has had sufficient practice with both the positive and negative sentences and perceives the pattern, continue with a more complex transformation drill, supplying the cue word not.

T — "The man is happy."
S — "The man is happy."
T — "Not..."
S — "The man is not happy."
T — "The girl is dancing."
S — "The girl is dancing."
T — "not..."
S — "The girl is not dancing."

As the student understands the positive/negative transformation, you might continue asking your student for more information.

Tutor shows picture of a boy holding a dog.

T — "Jimmy has a dog."
S — "Jimmy has a dog."
T — "not"
S — "Jimmy does not have a dog."

**Transformation Drill
Positive to Negative**

(pointing to pen)
T — "This is a pen."
S — "This is a pen."

(pointing to book and shaking head)
T — "This is not a pen."
S — "This is not a pen."

For more advanced students
(show picture of bus)
T — "This is a bus."
S — "This is a bus."

(show picture of motorcycle)
T — "not"
S — "This is not a bus."

Question patterns may be more difficult. When changing statements to questions, you can cue the student by holding up a card with a question mark on it. You may have to teach the ? symbol if it is not known, but most students know a question mark.

Model the sentence, having the student repeat it. Then restate it in a question form as you hold up a card showing a question mark.

T — "Harry is going to work."
S — "Harry is going to work."
T — (holding ? card) "Is Harry going to work?"
S — "Is Harry going to work?"

Model at least four sentences in this way. On the fifth, you might try giving the statement:

T — "Marie is reading a book." (Holding up the ? card as a cue) "Is...?"
S — "Is Marie reading a book?"

Eventually you'll model the statement and simply hold up the question mark.

T — George is climbing a tree.
(shows ?)
S — Is George climbing a tree?

**Transformation Drill
Statements to Questions**

T — (pointing to window) "This is a window."
S — "This is a window."
T — (holding ? card) "Is this a window?"
S — "Is this a window?"
T — (pointing to door) "This is a door."
(Tutor holds up ? card)
S — "Is this a door?"

Continue in the same pattern, substituting only one word, holding the rest of the sentence or phrase constant. You can do this with the different tenses in English not necessarily teaching your student the names of the tenses. Include the adverbs **today, yesterday, tomorrow** in the sentences to cue the correct response.

Past, Present and Future Drill

T — "Today I'm going to play tennis."
S — "Today I'm going to play tennis."
T — "...yesterday.."
S — "Yesterday I played tennis."
T — "...tomorrow.."
S — "Tomorrow I will play tennis."

BACKWARD BUILDUP

Often a sentence or even a word such as *refrigerator* is just too long for a student to repeat it correctly the first time. Usually, there is no problem at the beginning, but trouble starts near the end. Backward buildup provides practice in repeating long sentences.

In the following sentence, "We're going to the supermarket to buy some meat and vegetables for dinner", students often can repeat the first two phrases correctly, stumble over the third, and can't remember the fourth.

#1	#2
"We're going"	to the supermarket

#3	#4
to buy some meat and vegetables (problem)	for dinner (problem)

First, divide the sentence into phrases:
"We're going/ to the supermarket/to get meat and vegetables/for dinner."
Start on the **last** phrase, proceeding forward from there
T — "...for dinner."
S — "...for dinner."
T — "to buy meat and vegetables for dinner."
S — "to buy meat and vegetables for dinner."
T — "to the supermarket to buy meat and vegetables for dinner."
S — "to the supermarket to buy meat and vegetables for dinner."
T — "We're going to the supermarket to buy meat and vegetables for dinner."
S — "We're going to the supermarket to buy meat and vegetables for dinner."
There is more repetition of the phrases that caused most problems.

Because **you** can speak and understand English, these sentences give you no trouble. If you were trying to say them in a foreign language, the story would probably be different.

To get a "feel" for your student in this situation, try the following technique with a friend, using numbers. Use three numbers to equal one English phrase. Although your student had four English phrases, to make it easier, give only three "phrases" of numbers to your friend. Say the entire sentence (three sets of number phrases) at a normal speed.
"425-346-291"

Your friend will probably get "425-346..." (If your friend is **very** bright, he may get all three number phrases. If so, try it with four sets of numbers). Whether three or four sets of numbers are used, this illustrates the difficulty which often faces conversational English students.

The backward buildup technique helps the student to remember phrases long enough to put them all together:
T — "291"
S — "291"
T — "346-291"
S — "346-291"
T — "425-346-291"
S — "425-346-291"
You can use the backward buildup technique with basic students who have trouble with short sentences.
T — "Let's walk to the children's school."
S — "Let's walk to..."
T — "to the children's school."
S — "to the children's school."
T — "Let's walk to the children's school."
S — "Let's walk to the children's school."
This technique is especially helpful as your student repeats longer and longer sentences.

Backward Buildup

If your conversational English student has trouble repeating a complete sentence as modeled by the tutor, start the drill by using the *last phrase of the sentence.*

He went/ to work/ at six o'clock/
on Tuesday morning./

T — "...on Tuesday morning."
S — "...on Tuesday morning."
T — "...at six o'clock on Tuesday morning."
S — "...at six o'clock on Tuesday morning."
T — "...to work at six o'clock on Tuesday morning."
S — "...to work at six o'clock on Tuesday morning."
T — "He went to work at six o'clock on Tuesday morning."
S — "He went to work at six o'clock on Tuesday morning."

Dialogue

There are two kinds of dialogue exercises you will use in teaching conversational English. They are memorized dialogues and cued dialogues. Dialogues which are memorized are used with beginning students or to introduce new material. Cued dialogues are used with more experienced students, centered around a topic the student is familiar with, and using vocabulary the student knows.

MEMORIZED DIALOGUE

An effective way to present and practice the patterns and structures of English is to present them in dialogue rather than in isolation. You can incorporate all the techniques presented — substitution drill, response drill, transformation drills, and backward buildup.

A dialogue is a conversational exchange between two people in a given situation. A dialogue can be taken from an conversational English text or one which you have prepared yourself. You will help your student to memorize this dialogue through repetition and reponse drills. Even at a basic level, dialogues can somewhat resemble brief real-life conversations. Speak as you would speak normally. However, keep the sentences simple and limited to four lines at first.
T — "Will you have a cup of coffee?"
S — "Yes, thank you."
T — "Sugar and cream?"
S — "No, I take mine black."
First, say the entire dialogue, having your student listen. Perform any activities or use any objects or pictures to give meaning. By sitting in opposite chairs or by turning the head one way for each person, the tutor indicates she or he is one person for lines 1 and 3, and another person for lines 2 and 4.

When modeling the dialogue, be sure to speak as you would speak normally. Talk with normal speed and rhythm. Speak clearly but not too loudly. Present the whole dialogue twice before you ask the student to repeat. Next, say the first sentence, asking your student to repeat it several times until you're sure it can be said with fairly good pronunciation. Then do the same for the second sentence. You say it and have your student repeat it as often as necessary. Repeat this process for each sentence. You may have to repeat each line several times before your student is comfortable with it.

Now repeat the entire dialogue and have your student listen. Go through the dialogue having your student say each line with you. Repeat this until your student has the dialogue memorized. Check to see if your student understands the context and meaning of the dialogue.

Next, use the dialogue as conversation! You give the first line. Your student responds with the second line. Do this line by line until the student can do it easily.

Then reverse the roles and have the student give the first line while you give the second line and so on through the dialogue.

When the pattern is learned, you can substitute words such as *tea* for *coffee* or adapt the dialogue in some other way, keeping the same general pattern.

T — "Will you have a sandwich?"
S — "Yes, thank you."
T — "Lettuce and tomato or ham and cheese?"
S — "I'd like ham and cheese."

Often in a dialogue, the two parts are spoken by people with different roles in the situation. Although some conversational English students are waiters or waitresses, it is more likely that yours would be a customer in a restaurant. In such dialogues, be sure the student masters the part that is more "real". Do this by taking the part of the waiter or waitress yourself. Use pictures to "cue" the student to give more than one likely response. Again, use substitution drills to help the student give answers in good English.

You can employ dialogues to teach English that your student will actually use. What will your student need to say in the following situations?

1. An unexpected event prevents a lesson.
2. There's an emergency and a doctor must be called.
3. He or she is in a restaurant, and doesn't know how to order.
4. Directions aren't understood.

Write simple dialogues of your own for these situations.

It is very helpful to tape dialogue sessions for review at home. As the student repeats the sentences with the tape recorder, there is practice for the student in pronunciation as well as normal rhythm. The use of a tape recorder is an excellent way to teach idiomatic expressions which your student may encounter.

Here's a dialogue for a student who can master the simpler

dialogues without much trouble. In working on this dialogue you will probably use every technique. Because the sentences are longer the backward buildup technique will be useful. Pictures of a refrigerator, cheese, meat and bread would be helpful. The tutor, gesturing for the student to listen, says and act out the dialogue.

1 — "What's in the refrigerator? I'm hungry."
2 — "There's cheese, meat, and bread. Why don't you have a sandwich?"
1 — "Yes, that sounds good."
2 — "Why don't you make one for me, too?"
1 — "All right, I will."

With every dialogue, go through all the steps that we've recommended. In this dialogue, perhaps the tutor would find the student couldn't repeat the first line. This presents a perfect spot for backward buildup.

T — "I'm hungry."
S — "I'm hungry."
T — "What's in the refrigerator? I'm hungry."
S — "What's in the refrigerator? I'm hungry."

Using pictures, you can change the situation. Instead of a refrigerator, a cooler or picnic basket could be used. Other foods can also be substituted within the dialogue. Eventually the conversational English student can feel confident to use the expressions learned in dialogues with their own selection of vocabulary.

Write down the dialogues you use in your lessons for your own use. Re-teach them later. Go through them often.

Probably the most difficult thing for the tutor to realize is that there must be constant review and repetition. "Once over lightly" will not suffice! Remember, everything is new and much repetition is needed to build confidence as well as vocabulary.

Dialogues are worth all the effort of drill and practice. The fun comes when the two of you can use the device for real conversation. And it is reassuring indeed to your student to be able to understand and speak in a meaningful way.

CUED DIALOGUE

It is important that your student speak and understand in planned conversations, but your goal is to have your student converse spontaneously and in real-life situations. Cued or prepared dialogue can be an entrance into free dialogue or discussion.

An entertaining way to use dialogue is to take a sequence of cartoons and cut out the words.

Using the situation in the cartoon as the basis for a dialogue, you and your student decide what words you'd like the characters in the cartoon to say.

Role-playing, or situational learning, is an important tool in introducing and practicing cued dialogues, especially for the more advanced student. Set the stage for role-playing in a given situation. Perhaps your student will be visiting a school. You could pretend that you are the office receptionist, asking the appropriate questions. You might want to tape the entire dialogue and then play it back for both of you to review.

A list of common survival role playing situations might be: cashier-customer; bank teller and customer; nurse/doctor's assistant and patient; bus driver and passenger; pharmacist and customer; supervisor and employee.

Dialogue

Dialogue is a conversational exchange between two people. Incorporate all the techniques as they are needed. Keep the dialogue simple at first and keep it to four lines.

1 — "What's this?"
   2 — "It's an orange."
1 — "Do you like oranges?"
   2 — "Yes, oranges are good."

Steps for learning dialogue
1. Tutor says entire dialogue, being sure the student understands content/meaning.
2. Tutor says first sentence.
   Student repeats first sentence.
3. Tutor says each sentence
   Student repeats each sentence.
4. Tutor says entire dialogue
   Student listens.
5. Tutor and student say together the entire dialogue.
6. Dialogue: Tutor
            Student
            Tutor
            Student
7. Reverse the roles if appropriate.
8. Variations for further practice: substitute words or lines, especially on the tutor's part; add new lines for a longer dialogue; combine two, short related dialogues.

Creative Drills

These drills allow the student to use language more creatively. While there are many creative drills, just a few will be mentioned here.

SENTENCE COMBINING

Giving your student a chance to create more complex sentence structures from very simple sentences helps independent speaking. Begin with the student repeating after you.

   T — "Bob is tall. Bob is strong."
Gesture by bringing two hands or fingers together to suggest combining the sentence as you say:
   T — "Bob is tall and strong."

   S — "Bob is tall and strong."
After some repetition, your student will get the idea and will respond after hearing the two sentences and seeing you gesture.
   T — "The truck is rugged. The truck is expensive."
   S — "The truck is big and expensive."
Additional connecting words such as "but", "so", or "because" can be taught. Be sure to practice one at a time, with several sentences for each.
   T — " The building is five stories high. It is difficult to walk to the top floor."
   S — "The building is five stories high so it is difficult to walk to the top floor."
   T — "I burned my tongue. I drank hot coffee."
   S — "I burned by tongue because I drank hot coffee."

Sentence Combining

1. Tutor says two short sentences.
   T — The coffee is hot.
        The coffee is strong.

2. Student repeats.
   S — The coffee is hot.
        The coffee is strong.

3. Tutor gestures to combine them and says,
   T — The coffee is hot and strong.

4. Student repeats.
   S — The coffee is hot and strong.

Once this routine is comfortable for the student, use only steps 5 and 6. If this becomes difficult, return to steps 1 through 4 also.

5. Tutor models,
   T — "The coffee is hot. The coffee is strong."
        gesturing to combine.

6. Student says,
   S — "The coffee is hot and strong."

RESTATEMENT DRILL

For a student at Levels II or III of the conversational ESLOA Test (see Chapter 5), the Restatement Drill is helpful. Merely direct your student to start a sentence in a different form, such as:
   T — "Tell me you are going to the library."
   S — "I'm going to the library."
Remember to give several sentences of practice with the same form of restatement.
   T — "Tell me you are looking for a book."
   S — "I'm looking for a book."
   T — "Tell me you are reading stories to your child in English."
   S — "I'm reading stories to my child in English."
This is an effective way of encouraging your student to talk, without repeating what you say verbatim.

Another form of restatement drill is where the student asks the question:
   T — "Ask me where I went on vacation."

S — "Where did you go on vacation?"
T — "I went to New York City."

T — "Ask me when I went on vacation."
S — "When did you go on vacation?"

RESTATEMENT DRILL WITH GRAMMATICAL CHANGES

For advanced students, a special restatement drill can be used to introduce and reinforce more difficult features of English such as verb tense, etc.

The basic structure is:

"Today I'm having lunch with a friend."

Cue word — *yesterday:*

"Yesterday I had lunch with a friend."

Cue word — *tomorrow:*

"Tomorrow I will have lunch with a friend."

For an even more advanced student, these change drills are equally important. Ask your student to restate this sentence:

T — "Last week I saw an accident and got a call today to be a witness."

S — "You saw an accident last week and today you got a call to be a witness."

The student must remember the original sentence and create a new one, not merely repeat the original sentence. It must be reformed to be grammatically correct. Other restatement drills can be based on changing speech to a report of what was said. An example is:

T — "They told me to report to the employment office again in two weeks and not forget to bring my birth certificate with me."

S — "They told you to come back to the employment office in two weeks and to bring your birth certificate with you."

Restatement Drill

T — "When I went to the clinic today they gave me vitamin pills and told me not to forget to take one every day."

S — "Today when you went to the clinic they gave you vitamin pills and told you to remember to take one every day."

COMPLETION DRILL

Your student can get additional practice in forming correct sentences and a chance to be creative with the new language using a Completion Drill. The tutor starts a sentence and the student finishes it appropriately.

T — "I bought..."
S — "I bought a few oranges."

For the more advanced student, you should expect more.

T — "On the way to my lesson..."
S — "On the way to my lesson, I met two men from my country and we began talking."

Completion Drill

The tutor begins a sentence suggesting the student complete it appropriately.

T — "I have..."
S — "I have a new car."

SEQUENTIAL STATEMENT DRILL

For conversational English students who are able to understand spoken English fairly well, but freeze when asked to speak, the Sequential Statement Drill is suggested. The student repeats the sentence provided by the tutor, adding as many appropriate sentences as he/she can, with the content based on their own knowledge, experience, and imagination.

T — "I know an old man."

S — "I know an old man. He lives across the street from me, and is known to everyone. He enjoys watching the children play."

Sequential Statement Drill

1. Tutor says a sentence
   "I bought a used car."

2. Student repeats the sentence and adds as many appropriate sentences as possible.
   "I bought a used car. It's a blue 1982 Ford, four door. I got an excellent deal and it's in good shape."

SENTENCE UNSCRAMBLING

Sentence Unscrambling gives even a lower level student, but one who does a little reading, a chance to think about language. The tutor gives the student a list of words in random order, and the student has to arrange them in the right order to form a sentence. Of course, the tutor should choose words and sentence structures with which the student is familiar.

T — "sandwich, I, a, ordered."
S — "I ordered a sandwich."

The same technique can be used with the sentences of a dialogue you have studied. Write each line on a card or a strip of paper. Help the student read the lines and put the dialogue together. Or you could give a student who is more proficient in reading, a series of sentences and have him/her put them in the correct sequence. Cut apart a comic strip and have your student put the frames in the correct order.

Unscrambling Sentences Drill

Tutor gives words or sentences in random order and the student puts them in the proper sequence.

T — "vegetables, store, the, I, bought, at"
S — "I bought vegetables at the store."

Drills: General Tips

Introduce any new type of drill very simply and repeat it until your student understands the concept and sees the pattern. Repetition may seem dull to you, but to your student it builds confidence and gives much needed practice. It's a long road between saying something once, and having it come naturally in a conversation.

CHAPTER 9
Teaching Tools

Role Playing...Visual Aids...Bilingual Dictionary...Texts/Workbooks...Games

Role Playing

In planning your lessons, you will want to think about the everyday situations that your students face. With the use of a few props, you can act out ordinary situations with your students.

To begin planning, put yourself in your student's place. What does your student need to say in English? Where does the student go to use English? Think of the following situations, and then add your own, as occasions that demand the use of practical English:

1. Answering the telephone,
2. Asking directions,
3. Shopping in various kinds of stores,
4. Telling a doctor about pain or illness,
5. Ordering in a restaurant,
6. Visiting a friend,
7. Cashing a check at the bank.

Most people will find statements and questions involving food items of immediate use.. Although some of the words may be known, they may be pronounced incorrectly. Set up a demonstration with a few items and act out a grocery shopping situation.

Use the lists of "Compentency Based Mainstream English Language Training" (MELT) in Appendix A for more ideas for topics incorporating real life language skills needed by conversational English students. These lists were developed after years of experience by the Office of Refugee Resettlement, US Department of Health and Human Services, Washington, D.C.

To use the information in the lists to best advantage, look through them and compare the suggestions of topics and areas that people need to be competent in, with what you know of your student's needs and skill level. Then choose activities that will introduce the topic and develop it so that it becomes part of your student's language skills. Note that each list progresses within each topic from the simplest needed listening comprehension to more complex conversation production.

Planned dialogues in role-playing situations can prepare the student for real experiences. Spontaneous conversation is easier when you have identified specific topics of conversation. As your student progresses, you may wish to make trips to a store, to a restaurant, or to a park. A trip to the municipal market would be a fine learning experience. Your student would be given the opportunity to hear other voices speaking English beside yours, and yet you'd be there for support. Such a visit would provide many clues to the language needed for independence in everyday living.

The biggest problem the tutor encounters is getting the student to use English more often than during the time spent in lessons. Ingenuity in developing occasions to increase the amount and variety of English practice will speed the process of learning.

It's a good idea to rehearse language which might be used in a local real life situation. Perhaps a student is fearful of talking to the police because of past experiences. Discuss what your student wants to say, rehearse it with your student, and go with your student to talk with the police. This same procedure can be used in many areas.

Visual Aids

Tools for teaching conversational English are endless. Visual materials are an excellent way to promote communication, Giving your student the opportunity to associate words with actual objects, pictures or actions.

REAL OBJECTS

Lessons are easier if you have real materials to show the students as you use the relevant language. For instance when teaching the use of the telephone, use a real phone. If a real phone is not available, bring a toy phone to your teaching session and actually give your student numbers to practice. A cardboard phone dial or touch tone phone is not as good, but it still affords practice. Once your student knows how to dial or use a touch tone, give him/her your phone number and ask him/her to call you at a specific time. You might want to practice the common "phone courtesies" we use.

If you are teaching a lesson on how to start a bank account, bring deposit and withdrawal slips and if possible, an actual savings account passbook.

Any one needing to keep house for themselves or others will find statements and questions involving food items of immediate use. Although your students may know some of the words, they may pronounce them incorrectly. Set up a demonstration with a few items and act out a grocery shopping situation.

The most practical visual aids for building initial conversation are real objects such as may be found in your teaching room — table, chairs, window, pencil, book — whatever is available. Use all the objects in the room, using all techniques.

"Here's a chair."
"How many windows are there?"
"Is the door open or closed?"
"What color is my sweater?"

Bring in objects from home. Items which are common to your student's life can act as stimuli for conversation: a watch, articles of clothing, pots and pans, a transistor radio. There are endless questions to encourage conversation:

A handbag (handles, leather, mirror),
A sewing kit (needles. thread, scissors),

A box of cereal (box, cardboard),

An ashtray (glass, round).

Depending on the ability of your student, questions could include:

"What is it?"

"Where did it come from?"

"How long have you had it?"

"What is it made of?"

Gradually encourage the student to ask you these same kinds of questions. This will provide speaking practice and perhaps even meet your student's curiosity about American cultural concepts.

The more senses we employ, the more effective our teaching and learning. An actual orange has weight, fragrance, and color, and its name will be fixed in the student's mind through his senses of touch, sight, and smell. Use real objects whenever possible, but if you can't get real objects, use pictures. Bring a few props which will build interest and give meaning to new vocabulary.

PICTURES

Parts of the following are adapted from Ossoff, 1976

It is often difficult to bring real life situations into your teaching session without the use of pictures. They are the best substitute for actual objects and actions.

In teaching new words, even in a simple substitution drill, pictures can reveal a meaning immediately, making comprehension easy. Some books are now available that have only pictures. (See Recommended List, pg. 73). These are invaluable as a basic tool for teaching conversational English. You can adapt these to any drills, using them to teach structure or vocabulary. They can be adapted to lessons for students of any ability.

Pictures from catalogs, magazines, newspapers, calendars, advertisements, maps, photographs, post cards — all can be especially useful for teaching conversational English. It is wise to collect these illustrations before the need arises for a particular picture. A library of pictures is a valuable aid. The time and effort spent in collecting a variety of pictures is most rewarding as you plan your lessons. Once you start thinking about pictures as teaching tools for your conversational English student, collecting will become a "disease", and you will become a "clip-to-maniac", clipping everything in sight.

It is suggested that you file your pictures by topic for ready reference, mounting pictures on heavy paper or cardboard.

You'll soon discover that pictures generally fall into two categories:

1. Those illustrating a single object or action.

2. Those depicting an entire situation.

Both of these types are valuable. As you start to collect pictures, you may find the following suggestions helpful.

1. Cut out everything which you believe you can use. You can always discard those pictures which you don't need, but it is hard to locate those you wished you had cut out.

2. Select pictures which illustrate a single object, place, individual, group of people, scene, or action. These will constitute the bulk of your file. Pictures should be as simple as possible.

3. Collect pictures which depict an entire situation and can be used as a topic for conversation, for example, a family washing its car on a Sunday afternoon. These pictures can be used with students at any level. Pictures included in the file which depict different emotions such as love, hate, anger, fatigue, and so forth, are very useful.

4. Avoid using pictures which have printing on them. To a person who is unfamiliar with American culture and who knows little English, a labeled can of deodorant resembles labeled cans of other products: starch, hairspray, shaving cream, or furniture polish. As well as showing a picture of the container, show the object being used.

5. Although most of the pictures in your file will, and should, reflect American culture, try to include some which depict other lands and people. Your student will enjoy a conversation which is centered on a picture of a familiar object or scene. You should ask your students for any pictures they might like to bring to lessons and share.

6. Do not label the picture or write on the front of the picture. Write on the back. You might identify the subject matter (clothes — children's; or animals — cats) for filing purposes, or write notes for suggested use of the picture. Possible questions are always useful:

"What is the item on sale?"

"Where can you buy it?"

"Do you need it?"

"How much does it cost?"

7. Include pictures which illustrate contrasts, such as short-tall, big-small, happy-sad, wide-narrow, etc. Also, include pictures which illustrate concepts difficult to describe, e.g. above, under, between, up, down, either-or, numbers and colors.

Using pictures of individual objects, you can start with the response drill and later ask simple questions which can be answered by the student independently:

T — "What's this?"

S — "It's a bicycle."

T — "What color is the bicycle?"

You can use these pictures to stimulate a response in almost any drill. They are most valuable in teaching dialogue where you want the student to supply substituted words.

T — "We need vegetables to make a salad. What shall I get?"

S — "Carrots, tomatoes, and lettuce."

T — "What shall I get to make soup?"

S — "Potatoes, and onions, celery and carrots."

Pictures illustrating *fruit* would be an ideal tool to help in substituting vocabulary, or *groceries* or *children's clothes*. The ideas are endless.

Maps are another way that conversation can be stimulated. Bring a map of the world, of your student's country, of the USA or Canada, of your particular state or province, and then perhaps of your city or town with actual streets indicated. You can share information as you look at each map, learning from your student as you find out about his or her country, and teaching more about this country. On the town map ask your student to trace the route taken to get to some familiar place, meanwhile talking with you in English.

Picture books are available from various publishers, where only pictures, no words, are used. Tutors can use these just as they've used individual pictures.

You can go a bit further and use pictures showing various situations. Pictures can tell a story, such as a family eating dinner, a man and a boy fishing. These are invaluable aids to stimulating conversations. Depending on the ability of the student, you might ask these questions:

"How many people are in the picture?"

Or you might ask an inference question:

"Why do you think the boy is laughing?"

Pictures can open up not only areas of conversation but also areas of real need. If your student is contemplating buying a car or a refrigerator, get out your pictures and discuss the features to look for, the prices and terms of payment, etc.

Such a conversation could lead into a discussion of credit buying and financing. Not knowing what to expect or how to ask questions, students who speak little English may be talked into buying something which they don't really want, cannot afford, and do not really need. You could be doing a great service to your student if you include lessons of this type in your planning.

Don't overlook using pictures as you and your student role-play various situations. Pictures can help make any pretend dialogue nearly real.

SIMPLE DRAWINGS

You may sometimes want to draw a picture to help in teaching a word or an action or a concept that can't wait for a more artistic display. For example, if you are working on telling time and do not have a clock or picture, it is very easy to draw a clock and vary the hands.

You can make your own stick figures to illustrate a word or action. You need not be an artist to do this!

Why not give it a try?

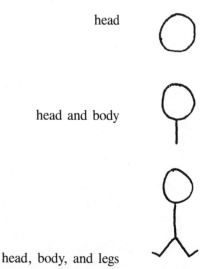

head

head and body

head, body, and legs

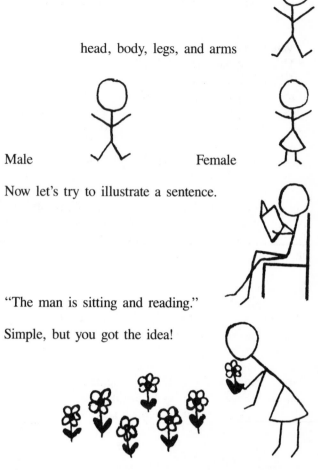

head, body, legs, and arms

Male   Female

Now let's try to illustrate a sentence.

"The man is sitting and reading."

Simple, but you got the idea!

"The woman picked the flower from the garden."

Note that since the action being described is in the past tense, your drawing must show the action completed. It's fun, you'll both laugh, and you will have communicated.

If you are fortunate enough to have funds for extra material, there are commercially made stick figure cards that are excellent.

ACTIONS

In learning a new language, it is very important that the conversation be related to **actions**. When you ask your student to open a window, have that student actually open a window in response. When a student is learning to use the future tense, telling you what he is going to do, is a real challenge.

S — "I'm going to sharpen my pencil."

It is important that the pencil be sharpened. Associating actions and time (future) are important. You can quickly get past tense by asking, "What did you do?" The reponse, "I sharpened my pencil" demonstrated understanding of past tense.

Don't hesitate to demonstrate words and phrases like *shaking hands, eating, standing, laughing*. Remember, the more senses we use, the more information we receive and the better we are able to remember. When your student responds and carries out the physical activity associated with the language, learning is more likely to be retained.

Bilingual Dictionary

Adapted from Ossoff,1976a.

One of the most frequently overlooked aids in the teaching of conversational English is the bilingual or two-way dictionary. The bilingual dictionary can prove to be an indispensable aid **if it is used with forethought and moderation.**

The bilingual dictionary should be an aid, not a crutch. Whenever possible the tutor should use actual objects and actions so that the student is encouraged to link the English word directly to the concept, avoiding translation as an intermediate step.

Abstract nouns such as *knowledge, beauty, and opportunity,* are quite difficult to explain by demonstration, pictures, simple definitions, or by just using the word in meaningful context. Here the bilingual dictionary might prove to be a very valuable aid. Use of the dictionary can also help the student learn such words as *alone, ago,* and *too.*

There are two basic approaches to using a bilingual dictionary. The method which you use will be determined primarily by the degree of literacy your student has in the native language and the system of writing used in that language (whether it has a non-Roman alphabet, etc).

1. For students who can read and write in their native language, the tutor locates the English word in the English part of the dictionary and shows that word in the native language.

2. For students who cannot read and write in their native language, the tutor can try to actually pronounce the word in the student's language, relying on the phonic regularity of that language to communicate the desired word.

Bilingual dictionaries can be very helpful but caution is advised in their use. Be sure you have the right part of speech, and if more than one definition is given, look it up in the other part of the dictionary to see what other English meanings are given.

The point is illustrated in the following story:

I was writing to my Spanish-speaking friend in Mexico. I wanted to begin the letter with the greeting which is traditional in our culture, "Dear Lupe."

I looked up *dear* in the Spanish-English dictionary where I found the Spanish words, *caro, cara.* Confidently I wrote:

Cara Lupe

It wasn't until months later that I learned that *cara* means costly or expensive, and thus, *dear.*

In writing back my Spanish friend used the correct word *querida.*

For most of the lesson, stick to spoken English. If you happen to know your student's language, occasionally it can be helpful to explain something in that language. Use the student's native language only when you cannot get an idea across in English. Not knowing the other language is not necessarily a handicap. Use a bilingual dictionary to identify the words you cannot explain.

Texts and Workbooks

You should have long-range plans for your students in-struction. A good conversational English text can provide the sequence for your activities and can be used both with students who can read and write as well as with those who can't. Beyond the text, be as creative as you like but use the text as a guide to help organize your program of instruction.

Look over several textbooks. See Appendix E for "Guidelines for Selecting a Textbook". You may feel more comfortable with one particular text, finding it more appropriate for *your* student. After you have chosen a textbook, use this as a guide for continued learning. One skill builds on another.

Textbooks necessarily must have printed words. But if you'll read the foreword or teacher's guide, most authors suggest that the lessons be introduced by conversational or aural-oral methods.

Review each lesson in a textbook before teaching, remembering the sequence recommended —

Listening and understanding,

Speaking,

reinforced by

Reading,

Writing.

A procedure for teaching individual lessons in textbooks for a student who can read and write in English might be:

1. Give a simple explanation of the lesson.

2. Read examples from the textbook, having your student listen and not look at the book. (Using visual clues may be helpful.)

3. Ask your student to repeat the examples.

4. Have your student open his book and *read* the same examples he has just heard and repeated. The pictures and words reinforce the oral sentences.

5. Have your student listen and respond verbally, not looking at the book, as you read the oral exercises.

6. Ask your student to read the exercises giving appropriate responses orally first, and then writing them.

7. Ask your student to read the responses from his own writing, giving you the opportunity to correct pronunciation, intonation, spelling, capitalization, and grammar.

If you've had your student write the reponses as homework, have him/her read them at the next lesson as review. Thus reading and writing were reinforcements to the listening and speaking skills.

Don't overlook using a textbook to help you plan oral lessons even before your student learns to read and write English. Your own simple written material such as word cards that students can read and copy can be used to help develop initial reading skills.

Games

Vary the drills to be practiced by using them in games. Create new games, using ideas from books or from your own experience, but be sure the activities are fun and simple enough so that your student is relaxed. Here are a few suggestions.

VOCABULARY GAMES

Ask your student to give the female or male counterpart

for the following words.

boy-girl	niece-nephew
man-woman	father-mother
groom-bride	brother-sister
aunt-uncle	son-daughter
actor-actress	waiter-waitress

Or you might ask for the plural:

boy-boys
girl-girls
man-men
woman-women

You can use the same idea with opposites:

tall-short
slow-fast
top-bottom
old-young
big-small
fat-thin

Don't be surprised if the lesson doesn't go as planned. One student gave *second hand* as the opposite of *new!*

Do not include too many new words at one session, and review those learned at the last lesson before adding new ones.

Here is an activity that reinforces listening comprehension as well as enlarging vocabulary. Decide on a specific area for vocabulary building: items in a kitchen, plants in a garden, or parts of a car.

If your student wants to know the vocabulary of kitchen items, make stick drawings of a table, a refrigerator, and a stove on small cards. Block off a large sheet of paper as follows:

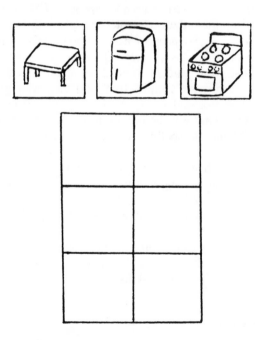

Ask the student to put the refrigerator in the upper left-hand square of the paper, the stove in the lower right-hand square, the table in front of the stove, etc. Make sure your student knows the meaning of *upper, left-hand, square* etc.)

A most useful activity for conversational English students is identifying the kinds of things one can buy at certain types of stores:

"What do you buy at a …
shoe store?
bakery?
post office?
jewelry store?"

"What can you buy at a drug store that you *cannot* buy at any other store?"

Students usually learn to say the colors correctly very soon. After your student is familiar with the English words for colors, use them in real situations:

"The traffic lights have _____, _____, and _____ lights."

"Nurses wear _____ uniforms."

"The colors of the flag of the United States are _____, _____, and _____."

"A blinking _____ light means proceed with caution, or go slowly."

COMMUNICATION GAMES

A communication game is one in which some people know something that the others don't know and where they must communicate in order to solve a problem or complete a puzzle.

The following is a communication game that two people can play. Player A and Player B sit back to back. Plastic figures or objects or pictures are in front of the players. Player A describes one of the objects or one of the pictures. Player B tries to identify the article or picture described. The only restrictions are that the person describing the object must use English, and the identifier must listen and identify the object in English.

Here is a variant on the refrigerator/location game mentioned above. One person (you or the student) has the pictures in place, but the other has only the pictures and they are not in place. Directions and questions must be used to locate equal pictures arrangement.

You also might adapt some of the old stand-by games that involve oral communication — "Hangman", "20 Questions", charade games, matching type games, Bingo, tic-tac-toe games.

Some conversational English students with traditional educational backgrounds may think games are only for children and resent using them in their lessons. Be sensitive to your student's reactions.

There are many books describing games and activities to use with your student. Include one game near the end of the lesson. Learning can be more fun with games.

Remember that in dealing with conversational English students, hard and fast rules rarely apply. There are as many second language student types as there are clouds in the sky. No two will fit into the same mold, and you will want to adapt even your games to your own particular students.

CHAPTER 10

Expanding Vocabulary

Vocabulary Development...Conversational Phrases...Student Word Lists

Vocabulary Development

In order to participate in and understand English conversations, your student will need an ever-expanding vocabulary for real competency in English. Instead of having the student memorize vocabulary lists, provide for the introduction of new words within a known structure, or compared to other, known vocabulary. Substitute new words in sentences and patterns you are working on. Be sure your student understands their meanings by using actions, objects, pictures, or the bilingual dictionary. For example, instead of teaching the following words in isolation, you could point to appropriate pictures and put the words in sentences:

coat

hat

shirt

tie

"He's wearing a coat."

"He's wearing a hat."

"He's wearing a shirt."

"He's wearing a tie."

As the student speaks, new words are being added and used correctly in context. This is much more effective than having the student repeat word lists.

As you and your student search for meaningful vocabulary, you might:

(1) Talk about a picture and identify three or four words to be learned.

(2) Ask "yes" and "no" questions about a vocabulary item.

(3) Ask a question which gives the student a choice of single word answers, e.g., "Is this a spoon or a fork?"

(4) Ask the student to produce the vocabulary, e.g. "What is he doing?"

(5) Reinforce the vocabulary just learned by using pattern drills, role playing or games.

For a more advanced student, sequential pictures that tell a story are helpful.

(1) Ask your student to tell you what is happening.

"The small dog sits on the grass."

"The small girl (he gestures) is bouncing a ball."

(2) Repeat the student's explanation but put it in standard English.

"The small dog is sitting on the grass."

"The small girl is playing with a ball."

(3) Ask the student to repeat the corrected sentence.

(4) Write down the sentences and ask that the sentences be repeated aloud.

(5) Read the sentences into a tape recorder, as a model.

(6) Have your student repeat the sentences with the tape recorder. He/she can then review the entire lesson at home.

When teaching new vocabulary, it is helpful to teach words in groupings.

1. Words associated with particular situations, such as *doctor, clinic,* and *medicine,*

2. Words illustrated by pictures, or objects at hand such as *table, chair, purse, door,*

3. Words which are related such as *act, acting* and *actor.*

Illustrate the new word in a sentence rather than defining it. Meaning will come by associating the new word with known English words, e.g.:

"A person who works for a company is an *employee.*"

"The person who hires him is his *employer.*"

"A person who has a job is *employed.*"

or,

"Good *health* is everyone's goal."

"A *healthy* diet helps to keep us well."

"Fruit is a *healthful* food."

Conversational Phrases

As your student progresses, make a list of everyday, practical questions and answers that might be needed. Making such a list is practical, stresses structure as well as introduces needed vocabulary:

"What time is it?"

"Where is the bus stop?"

"Where is the shopping center?"

"Why are you late?"

If, in responding, your student uses the wrong word order, or adds a word in his/her native tongue or leaves a word out, what can you do? If your student says,

"He going to es school,"

don't be bothered much by *es school.* In Spanish, all word initial "s" consonant blends are preceded by the syllable "es" — "escuela" (school), "estilo" (style). This is a pronunciation problem that is hard to correct at first. It is important that part of the verb, an essential part of the sentence, was omitted. *Do correct that.*

You might want to use the contraction as a basis for a short drill.

"He's going to school."

"I'm going to school."

"She's going to school."

"They're going to school."

Using pictures as a guide, you can substitute other words and create other structures.

"Where is she going tomorrow?"

"She's going to the library."

"Where is he going tonight?"

"He's going to the movies."

As you teach conversational English, you are working for sentence structure and word order familiar to the ear, not grammatical rules stored in the brain. Stress those concepts which follow regular patterns even as you introduce new vocabulary:

tall, taller, tallest

big, bigger, biggest

Maybe your student will come up with logical answers that will make you chuckle:

cold, colder, below zero

bad, worse, rotten

This indicates how much English they may have picked up already. Help them to use the English their ears are familiar with.

Often a student will have heard an English expression but will not know the component ends or structure.

"Whaya doon?"

"What are you doing?"

These expressions may take patience on your part to help the student figure out the meaning but keep at it. "Who said it?" "When?" Help your student to understand what the words are.

Student Word List

You might record the student's spoken vocabulary by using a word list. It is generally agreed that if a new word is retained on three separate days, the word is known. Mark the words your student uses in this fashion:

✓ = word said correctly without having heard it modeled (from picture, action, etc.)

✓✓ = word said correctly at two lessons
✓✓✓ = student knows the word.

refrigerator ✓
stove ✓✓
table ✓✓✓
chair ✓✓✓

When the student can use the new vocabulary words in his/her own sentences, you can be assured there is growth toward independent speech.

CHAPTER 11
Reading and Writing

**Sequence of Skills...Types of Students...Prereading and Writing Activities...
Teaching Initial Reading... Reading Comprehension...Expanded Reading**

Sequence of Skills

A useful sequence for teaching the four skill areas is:
Listening,
Speaking,
Reading,
Writing.

This sequence is particularly useful for beginning language students, especially those that are non-literate. For students literate in their own language or for Level III/IV students, you can sometimes use written material like a story or a newspaper article earlier. Progress in reading and writing will depend on individual students' experiences, education and abilities.

Because you want to reinforce the listening and speaking skills with reading and writing as soon as possible, you should integrate teaching reading and writing as you teach some of the conversational skills. However, when you are working with students who cannot speak English at all or who have problems understanding and communicating in English, it's best to delay having them read and write a lot of material in English. That is, give them materials to read and write that they have already learned orally. Thus, greetings, sentences used in substitution and response drills and in dialogues can be written for them to see and read. You could also teach them to write their names, addresses, phone numbers. It is a good idea to give students their words on cards to use for practice and recall between classes. This use of reading is actually for rehearsal of new vocabulary words and phrases. This then reinforces oral language.

When using a textbook, follow the same procedure of having your student read the material and write the answers *after* he/she's heard, understood, and said them.

Types of Students

When considering teaching reading and writing to your conversational English students you have to consider the fact that there are three different groups of conversational English students. They are:

Group A — Those conversational English students who cannot read and write in any language.

Group B — Those conversational English students who cannot read or write a language using the Roman alphabet, but can read and write their own language which uses a non-Roman alphabet or writing system such as Arabic, Chinese, or Thai.

Group C — Those conversational English students who can read and write using the Roman alphabet, but not English such as French, Spanish, or German.

For students in Group A, reading and writing will be most difficult and they will need special help. They will be learning to read for the first time in a language other than their own. Be sure to extend extra patience to these students.

Students in Group B will also have difficulty. Transfer of reading and writing skills from one form of script to another is not easy. Such students may be easily frustrated with their own good habits of letter formation and reading that simply don't apply in English.

Students in Group C will probably progress faster for they have many easily transferable skills. Still, it is a new language they are learning, and the sounds of English are not spelled the same way as in their language.

Pre-Reading and Writing Activities

You, and probably everyone you know, can read and write and learned to do so at an early age. Adults with the double disadvantage of speaking little or no English and being unable to understand written words in any language will need special help to learn basic reading and writing skills. Students with no or limited reading ability in any language will need patient guidance in order to learn the following skills and concepts:

The following points to remember when teaching reading are offered by Jeffrey Bright, Chicago Urban Skills Institute:

1. Print carries meaning.

2. The elements of print (letters, numerals, spaces, punctuation marks, etc.) are limited in number.

3. Text goes from left to right, line by line, from top to bottom.

4. Print is situated on imaginary (or drawn) horizontal lines.

5. Letters are separated by small, regular spaces, words are separated by larger, regular spaces.

6. Small differences in letter/numeral parts, shape or orientation are important. (Compare *d* with *b, e* with *c, h* with *n; 6* with g).

7. Each capital letter corresponds to a small letter and vice versa. Whether in capitals or lower case letters, a given word is the same.

8. Capital letters occur either throughout a word (or line), or only at the beginning of a line (or word.)

9. Sounds of English words are represented by a fairly complex but mostly regular system of letters and letter combinations.

These and other key concepts and skills are taken for granted by those of us who can read. But they are new for the pre-literate (Group A) or non-Roman alphabet student. Often it takes much longer than expected for the pre-literate student to learn to read. This is despite the fact that many students can learn oral English relatively fast. If your student is in this category, you may want to refer to **Tutor** (Colvin, Root, 1984), **Handbook for Volunteer ESL Literacy Teachers** (Kuy, Thomas) or other books on teaching basic reading. The references in Recommended Reading at the end of this book will also be of help.

Teaching Writing as Part of Reading

More and more research is demonstrating that learning to read and write at the same time speeds up the learning of both skills. "Writing" under these instructional circumstances can mean something as simple as copying a signature, or a phrase or a needed shopping list or it could mean the attempt to write something of interest that has happened to an individual student and used for a language experience activity. (See Language Experience below.)

As you teach your students to write, be aware of several important things about the conventions of our writing system.

To be able to write even fairly well in English, one must understand simple punctuation rules such as that sentences start with a capital letter and end with a period. Teach other details of punctuation as they are needed. Spelling in English is often confusing. Some words are phonically regular and others must be memorized. Assure your student that you can work together as he/she progresses.

Ask your student to tell you what kinds of writing are most important to him/her.

If your student has school age children, he/she will probably need to write simple notes to the teacher. A student who works in an office may need to understand and write simple messages. Writing checks or shopping lists may be what your student needs help on first.

If a student writes in a non-Roman alphabet or if he/she cannot read or write in his/her own language even if it has a Roman alphabet, his/her writing skills probably will develop slowly. Teach him to *write* individual letters, as you teach letter names. Continue with simple words and sentences he's learned orally. To the eyes of many students, cursive writing is more "adult." Remind them that printing is required on forms. With pre-literates or slow students, cursive writing is suggested only for the signature.

The same drills used in teaching conversational English can be adapted to writing. Substitution drill sentences give opportunities to write the same words again and again for practice and yet add new words. Transformation drills, sentence completion, sentence unscrambling — all can be done in writing. This leads to writing simple paragraphs and short stories.

Eventually you will want your student to practice composition, the writing of longer texts, allowing for expression of personal ideas and fulfilling practical needs. Have him/her practice writing different kinds of letters — job applications, letters of complaint, personal letters. Suggest he/she re-write something read, or he/she could "write" his/her experience story. This will give an opportunity to set down on paper the full range of his/her ideas, thoughts, and feelings.

Teaching Initial Reading and Writing

Your student should learn to read different kinds of material in English. The major source of reading materials for an conversational English student are:

1. Print material encountered in the real world.

2. The material of conversational English lessons you prepare.

For students who do not have pre-reading skills and for those who do not know any English, reading will probably be limited to your lesson material. Be aware that there are signs or labels that your students must read as they live day to day. Include them in your lessons. They need to read in order to survive and function in our complex society. Only give them materials to read and write that they have already learned orally. Thus greetings, sentences used in substitution and response drills and dialogues, can be written in manuscript (or in cursive, if your student can read cursive writing) or typed for him/her to see and read. This then reinforces oral language.

Your students want to learn to read and write independently, and you can help them acquire skills in word recognition. Because people learn in different ways that are not always predictable or completely understood, instructions can often be most effective by using several approaches at the same time. Some people seem to learn words as a whole. Many words in English should be learned this way because they do not break down readily into sound units. Other words can be recognized through the analysis of letter clusters. Four techniques will be described in this chapter:

1. Language Experience,
2. Sight Word and Context Clues,
3. Phonics,
4. Word Patterns.

However, you will have to adapt the techniques to the ability and needs of *your* student.

LANGUAGE EXPERIENCE

The experience story is an expression in the student's own words of a personal experience, a retelling of a news item, a description, a situational picture, a comment on a public happening, or anything of interest at the moment.

In the Language Experience technique, the student's oral language is put into print. To see one's own words written down provides the best of all possible motivations, for it is an individual's own story. It also gives the tutor insights into the student's world that can be a guide in selecting other materials.

Invite your student to talk — to tell you something of interest: why he/she came to America, something about his/her country's history, or his/her dream for the future or talk about an issue he's facing (looking for a job) or a problem he's dealing with (a difficult landlord). Alternatively, if the student fails to talk, use pictures deliberately. This makes the questioning less personal and less threatening. Try to get the student to express his/her thoughts in best spoken English. Encourage them to tell the same "story" again. Tell your student that you'll write his or her story in English.

Using manuscript writing (see alphabet in manuscript and cursive writing, at the end of this chapter) take down the words being spoken. Make a carbon copy for yourself.

"America is my new country, but Portugal is my home country. I make new friends but I miss my old friends."

Read aloud the student's entire message, pointing to each word. Then re-read the first sentence, again pointing to each word. Ask the student to read that sentence. Continue with the same procedure until he/she reads the story fairly well.

The student is now ready to begin learning to read his/her own words "out of context", separate from the story. Ask which words from the story he/she'd like to learn. Teach these words as sight words, using quartered 3 x 5 cards.

You can adapt this approach in many ways, having your student give you orally anything of a personal interest or concern, using that material as reading material. Because many students are still unfamiliar with English, and because you don't want to teach incorrect grammar or sentence structure it is often necessary to rewrite stories before having the student learn to read them. The more you can get the student involved in correcting his own grammar, the more involved in learning he/she will be.

A Spanish-speaking social worker wanted me to to help write a report to be read to the case conference group of which she was a member. She knew her English was inadequate. Here is what she dictated:

I have big problem in community. Is about one mother. She have six children. She have husband, too. She not well of the mind. She no feeling well in mind and she go to hospital to get especial attention medicine. We have problem of children now. Maybe one child go live with family Espanish. We calling at the last meeting. We not sure about that. Two of the children espeak English. The mother espeaks only Espanish. The rest only Espanish.

The rewritten story came out like this:

I have a big problem in my community. It is about a mother. She has six children and a husband, too. She is not well mentally. She goes to the hospital to get special medical attention. We have the problem of the children now. The mother speaks only Spanish. Two of the children speak English. The rest speak only Spanish. Maybe one child will go to live with a Spanish family. We were calling at the last meeting about that. We aren't sure what will happen.

The student was then asked to read the rewritten story. She was delighted and copied it as her report for the case conference.

SIGHT WORDS AND CONTEXT

Sight words may be defined as those words which the student should recognize immediately. There are several types of words which may be taught by having the conversational English student memorize the whole word.

1. Necessary words for which the student does not yet have the skills to decode any other way such as names of streets and towns (e.g. Main), job related vocabulary, and survival sign words (e.g. Danger, Bus Stop)

2. Basic words that are extremely common, (e.g. *the, of, no, for*).

3. Words that are not phonically regular, that is, their letter patterns do not follow sound patterns,(e.g *do, there, laugh*).

Teach sight words in the context of your lessons. These words may be taken from the dialogue or game you plan to use.

Before the lesson make a set of cards for the words you wish to teach. Limit new sight words to five for most students. 3 x 5 cards cut into quarters are convenient for teaching sight words. Print one word on each card. If your student writes in cursive, you can write the same word in cursive on the other side of the card.

Choose one word to learn, writing that word on a card; for example, the word *were.* Put it in a sentence: "The boys were going to the soccer game." The tutor shows the word card to the student and says:

T — "This word is *were.* What is the word?"

S — "Were."

T — "Look at this word closely. Again, what is the word?"

S — "Were."

If your student can write Roman letters, have him write the word.

After the student has successfully identified the first word, select another word and teach this in the same way. After five words have been learned, mix the cards and have the student read the words from the cards. Additional words and additional cards can be added at each lesson.

Sight words may be taught on the spur of the moment as well. You cannot always predict what your conversation with the student will be. So, have some blank 3 x 5 cards at each lesson. After, or sometimes during, a conversation, you or your student can select important new words. Teach them as sight words. Use your oral English lessons as teachable moments for literacy/reading instruction, reinforcing new words.

Since the student will meet many of these words at every turn, instant recognition is important in the reading experience. There are lists of sight words available in the appendix of TUTOR.

This same procedure can be used with words within your student's language experience as well.

Sight words can be used in sentence unscrambling or sentence building activities. If you find that your student makes a sentence but a word is missing, such as *a* or *of,* make a sight word card on the spot. Sight word reading can reinforce the student's learning of standard English.

PHONICS

Phonics is the study of the systematic relationship of letters to their sounds.

There are many ways to teach phonics. Any way is acceptable if it works with your student. The important thing is that the student associate sounds with letters and groups of letters.

The student who is not literate in any language will find this most difficult, while the student who can read and write in his own language, especially those with Roman letters, will probably know some names and appropriate sounds of many English letters. If your student cannot write Roman letters, you might want to teach letter name before teaching sounds. Letter recognition is a pre-reading skill. To teach letter names and the sounds they make at the same time may be very confusing, especially for students in Groups A and B as decribed above.

Because consonants in English are constant and vowels

are not, begin with consonants. Begin by teaching consonants that can be maintained in the initial position in a word, e.g. the letters *s*, *f* and *m*.

You should be thoroughly familiar with the instructional procedures before you begin teaching your student.

In the teaching examples that follow, letters are shown as *s, f*; sounds are shown as /sss/, /fff/.

You will be creating a letter-sound dictionary with your student as you proceed with the instructions that follow. Provide one sheet of paper or one 3 x 5 card for each letter, using the following format for teaching consonants.

Teaching Initial Consonants

Action	Tutor Says	Student Says
1. Tutor writes *s* in manuscript, points to it.	This is an *s*.	

```
s
```

2.	What is the name of this letter?	*s*
3.	Listen for the sound of *s* at the beginning of these words — sun, sink, socks, sandwich. Do your hear the sound?	(hopefully) *yes*
4.	You say these words after me —	

	sun	*sun*
	sink	*sink*
	socks	*socks*
	sandwich	*sandwich*
	sail	*sail*

5.	Which of these *s* words — *sun, sink, socks, sandwich, sail* — do you like best? (Often a key word will mean more if the student can identify with it. When picking a key word, it is better not to use a consonant blend such as *sn* in *snake* or *tr* in *tree*. It is easier for the student when you use a word with a single consonant beginning.)	(Student selects a word. Let's assume the word *sun* was selected.)
6. Tutor writes student's key word in manuscript under *s*.	*Sun* is your key word to help you remember the sound of *s*.	
7.	Think of the beginning sound in *sun*. Notice how you hold your lips, tongue and teeth. Now, let out just the first sound.	/sss/

```
s
sun
```

Action	Tutor Says	Student Says
(If the student, within a reasonable time, fails to make the desired response, supply it).	/sss/ is the sound of the letter s.	
8.	Here are some words. Listen. Do these words start with the s sound:	
	sausage	yes
	forest	no
	Monday	no
	salad	yes
	summer	yes
9.	Now, let's move this sound to the end of the word. Listen to the last sound in these words, and repeat the words:	
	gas	*gas*
	kiss	*kiss*
	bass	*bass*
10.	What is the last sound in these words?	/sss/
11. Tutor points to s.	What is the name of this letter?	s

s
Sun

12. Tutor points to sun.	What is your key word?	sun
13.	What is the sound of s?	/sss/
14. Student writes as tutor points. (A beginning student may need more writing practice of individual letters, using your manuscript letters as models.)	Will you write an s right here?	

s   s
Sun

| 15. Tutor prints capital S. | This is a capital S — the same name, the same sound. You use a capital letter to begin a person's name and to begin a sentence. | |

s   s
Sun   S

(If your student already writes in cursive, you should write the s and S in cursive, too.)

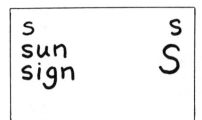

(More written words can be added to the s page later. It is helpful to have a newspaper or ·magazine available in which the student can circle all small or large s's. He may want to cut out the s words, and add them to the s page.)

Your student has a new skill that can be applied immediately. Suggest looking for the letter s on bus signs, street signs, and at work. Make it a part of daily observance.

Most important, have your student read again and again the name of the letter, the key word, and the sound. It is sometimes helpful to have a picture representing your student's key word. but do not permit dependence on pictures too long and do not use pictures other than the word for a key word. Be sure that the key word for s is the first word on your student's s page.

Some letters when put together have a special sound or sounds. When teaching the letters *sh, ch, th,* and *ng,* use the same format but pointing out that the two letters together have one sound. Just one word of caution: Work on phonics can become monotonous, so don't spend more than 10 minutes in one lesson on it.

PHONICS (CONSONANTS)

1. Identify letter.
2. Listen to beginning (or initial) sound.
3. Pick a key word.
4. Produce beginning sound.
5. Recognize sound in other words.
6. Put sound at end of words.
7. Produce ending sound.
8. Review — name of letter, key word, sound.
9. Write letter.

WORD PATTERNS

Vowels are the biggest problem in learning to read because a vowel can represent more than one sound. Frequently the sound the vowel represents can only be determined by noting the letters that follow it. Note the many ways "a" can sound in various patterns:

can
car
cake
call

Because of this, we do not teach vowel sounds in isolation.

Learning words in pattern the *word family way,* enables the student to readily see the relationships between clusters of letters and the clusters. Here are samples of two word families or patterns:

cap	loss
rap	toss
lap	boss
nap	moss

Parts of words that sound alike are often spelled alike. The spelling of the vowel sound is particularly hard to predict but becomes much more reliable when considered as part of a spelling pattern which includes the letters following the one representing the vowel.

Stop and think. Are you sure what a short "i" sound would be? Perhaps not, but few people would hesitate when asked to pronounce "-ip" or "-ig". Therefore, the instructional methods which will be described will not emphasize such things as long and short vowels and their related sounds. Instead, the letter clusters such as "-ad", "-og", "-im" will be the unit to be learned. Because of the irregularities of the English spelling system, even the student who reads and writes a language that uses our Roman alphabet will need special instruction in word families Here is a technique for teaching word patterns.

Teaching Patterned Words

Action	Tutor Says	Student Says
1. Tutor writes *at*	This word is *at*. What is this word?	*at*

```
at
```

2. Tutor writes *mat* directly under *at*.	if *a-t* is *at,* what is *m-a-t*?	*mat*

```
at
mat
```

(If there is no answer or an incorrect answer, supply *mat*.)

3. Tutor writes *sat*	And what is *s-a-t*?	*sat*

```
at
mat
sat
```

4. Tutor writes *fat*.	And what is *f-a-t*?	*fat*

```
at
mat
sat
fat
```

A word of caution. We have emphasized that beginning conversational English students should be taught to read only words which have been mastered orally. Because their vocabularies are limited, many words you'd like to use in pattern will be unknown to them, so use this technique with care.

At this point, you may want to reinforce the spelling of the words by their letter names. Ask your student to give the names of the letters in the words — a-t, c-a-t, s-a-t, f-a-t.

Keep this spelling review separated from the reading of the word patterns.

Reading Comprehension

Some people can read "words" but have no idea what they mean. You cannot presume your student understands what is read unless that student can put the meaning of the sentence into his own words.

Merely repeating words from a book may conceal a comprehension difficulty. Testing, not only in reading the words, but in comprehension as well, reveals much to a tutor.

Read the following sentences containing words you do not know, and answer the questions:

"The gorkle took the maisly furkles to the blinto."
Q — "Who took the furkles to the blinto?"
A — "The gorkle."
Q — "Where did the furkles go?"
A — "To the blinto."
Q — "What kind of furkles were they?"
A — "Maisley furkles."
Q — "What is a gorkle, a furkle, a blinto?"
A — "????"

You could score 75% on that test and have very little understanding of what you read. Mere repetition of the words of the book does not indicate literal comprehension.

It is suggested that you discuss together the content of an article to be read, perhaps asking questions before you have your student read, giving him an opportunity to think ahead. "Read this and tell me where Mrs. Jones is going." You can ask questions after a sentence, a paragraph or after the entire story has been read.

For more advanced students, you can ask questions requiring his drawing an inference. "Why do you think Mrs. Jones wants to go there?"

Another way to check reading comprehension is to use the Cloze procedure. A student reads a passage. He is then given a copy of the same passage with certain words deleted, replaced by blanks. The student fills in the blanks. Any word which makes sense is acceptable. In this example every fifth word is deleted.

Learning to care for their first baby is a big job for most adults. When their children are twins, it's often a giant challenge. Which one should you feed first when they both wake up ravenous at the same time? And which one should you rock when new teeth make them fussy at the same instant?

Learning to care for _____ first baby is a _____ job for most adults. When their _____ are twins, _____ often a giant challenge. _____ one should you feed _____ when they both wake _____ ravenous at the same _____? And which one should _____ rock when new teeth _____ them fussy at the _____ instant?

True or false statements can also check your student's understanding of a passage.

It is easier to care for twins than a single baby.
           True   False
You must decide which to feed first.
           True   False

A student will need help with new vocabulary words encountered in the passage. A matching activity can help to check and develop comprehension. Each word in Column A has a similar meaning to one in Column B.

A	B
challenge	hold close
ravenous	unhappy
rock	difficult job
fussy	very hungry

You might encourage your student by letting him practice these exercises *before* he reads the story.

Asking your student to complete sentences about a passage requires comprehension.

New teeth make a baby _____.
Rocking a baby helps when _____.

You can check comprehension by asking your student to re-tell the story in their own words, or by asking appropriate questions. Often there are questions at the end of an article or story.

If your student has trouble with the meaning of individual words, you can always refer to a bilingual dictionary. But encourage him to try to understand the meaning of the new word from the context first.

Comprehension of word meanings is the heart of language learning. Little is accomplished when a word can be read and pronounced correctly, but its meaning is obscure to the student. We must realize, however, that without certain background information, without understanding much in America's customs and culture, comprehension of what is said is often not complete.

Because of the importance of comprehension, no lesson should be considered completed until the tutor is satisfied that the words, phrases and sentences are completely clear to the student. Comprehension is an integral part of language learning.

Expanded Reading

As a student progresses in both oral and reading competence, he or she will be able to handle unfamiliar reading material, material he hasn't mastered orally. New vocabulary words, and even new sentence structures, can now be introduced in printed form. Silent as well as oral reading is encouraged. Silent reading allows the student to concentrate on reading for meaning rather than pronouncing words.

You might select several articles, describing them to your student, giving the **student** the opportunity to choose one of particular personal interest. It would be helpful to discuss new vocabulary, although he might get the meaning of new word through the context of the story.

Sometimes students have trouble understanding what they read because they don't understand how words go together. Break each sentence into phrases by putting slash marks in pencil after words that should be read together. Ask your student to look at the words between slash marks before he speaks any of them. Often he will have to say them to himself or "think" the words before he can say them together in a normal speech rhythm.

Some people say,/ "You can pick your friends,/ but you're stuck/ with your relatives."

Or you can rewrite the selection "one phrase per line", grouping the words together in structural units.

Some people say,
"You can pick your friends,
but you're stuck
with your relatives."

This technique can be adapted to any material your student is reading. Be sure the individual words are known before going into phrase reading. You can lengthen the groupings as he becomes more proficient.

As your student advances you can use this technique to help in comprehension if this is a problem. Call the student's attention to the fact that each group of words contains an idea and suggest restatement of those ideas in his or her own words.

To keep your student from getting discouraged by reading beyond his or her ability, it's best that **you** plan the reading books, **you** combine the reading with vocabulary study, **you** help in recognition of grammatical patterns, **you** follow up closely with comprehension exercises. You're building up to the next step: reading done on the student's own for individual purposes. Even now, your student may ask for help occasionally. The goal of independent reading has nearly been reached.

Reading should be a growing part of your lesson plans, especially integrating it with practical situations. For example, if you've worked on starting a bank account or writing a check, an advanced student could include "reading" the various forms—withdrawal slips, credit loans, etc. If part of a lesson was on medical matters, an advanced student might "read" instructions on use of specific medicines. A sports fan might "read" articles from a sports magazine or the sports section of the paper. More and more reading can be done by your student independently, using listening, speaking, reading and writing in his or her new English, each one reinforcing the other.

****

Now the sequence of learning a language is complete. When your student can listen and understand, can speak so that others can understand him, can read and write, he's well on his way to independence in his new language, English.

Manuscript Alphabet

a b c d e f g h i j k l m n o p
q r s t u v w x y z

A B C D E F G H I J K L M N O P
Q R S T U V W X Y Z

Cursive Alphabet

a b c d e f g h i j k l m n o p q r s t
u v w x y z

A B C D E F G H I J K L M N O P Q R S T
U V W X Y Z

CHAPTER 12
Especially for the Level III And IV Student

All the techniques given in the previous chapters can be adapted to more advanced students. Tutors sometimes feel inadequate with the Level III or IV student, and hesitate to use basic drills. However, they can be very effective with the more advanced students. Here are some specific suggestions:

Pictures

Bring several pictures to the lesson. For the advanced student, suggest:

"Describe the girl in the upper right corner"

or

"Tell me how you feel about this picture."

If your student can write in English, you could ask your student first to give you his reply orally. Then suggest he write it down. However, if your student is hesitant about writing in English, write down the reply and review it together later. Or you could tape the reply, using the information as a base for further conversation. Such spontaneous expression gives you an opportunity to see if there are words that your student does not know, as well as giving you an opportunity to check if either the student's vocabulary or grammar is not correct, model the sentences correctly, and make a note on your Error Chart to review the errors at the next session.

Inter-Active Listening/Speaking

Another activity for students in Levels III and IV involves both listening and speaking. Choose a picture that shows a situation, or even a topic for which there is no picture. You could suggest topics such as "My Family" or "A Bad Day at Work", or your student could suggest several topics. If it is something that both the student and the tutor are interested in that is good, but of primary importance is the student's interest.

Give a short spontaneous talk about the picture or the topic, perhaps about 8-10 normal sentences. Speak as you normally would to an English-speaking friend. This will be a challenge to the advanced student.

Invite your student to ask clarification questions. Questions could be "What does _____ mean?" "Did you say you liked _____?" Then, talk again, reviewing your conversation. Don't worry if your words are different. Just stick to the same ideas. Your student will have this second chance to reinforce his listening skills.

If your student needs no further clarification ask him to retell the same conversation in his own words. If you tape record your version as well as your student's version, you'll have another chance to listen and discuss this sample of natural language. (adapted from Clark)

Discussion

Questions are helpful tools to use to solicit information about your student, to get him or her to talk. But just as important, your student must learn how to ask questions to get information.

You might want to use this method to prod an advanced student to ask questions (adapted from Zuck, 1972). Bring one object with you to your tutoring session on which to focus attention. It could be something as ordinary as a transistor radio, a container of spice, or a tennis ball.

To open the conversation, you might say:

"This is a transistor radio. We take it with us when we go to the beach."

or...

"This is a can of nutmeg. Nutmeg is a spice I use a lot in cooking."

or...

"This is a tennis ball I used in a game last weekend."

You can solicit information from your own questions:

"Why do you think I brought this radio (or nutmeg or tennis ball) with me today?"

If your student doesn't respond, you could encourage further conversation by answering the question yourself:

"I brought it to talk about — to have you ask questions about it."

Then wait for your student to ask the questions. You give the answers.

A good portion of the lesson could be directed around the radio, nutmeg, or tennis ball, including new vocabulary words.

If you brought a tennis ball, words could be *tennis, court, sneakers, scoring, racket, net* - and could continue on to a discussion of the sports in your student's country. You could use all your drills, focusing on tennis. A continuation of this lesson (if the student is interested) could include asking the student to bring in a newspaper, magazine article, or pictures about tennis. The discussion could take any direction — sports for health, famous tennis players, how sporting equipment is made, where tennis is played.

The second lesson could reinforce the same vocabulary with new information your student has gathered about tennis. Have pictures and reading material available for further saturation on the one subject matter. You may want to spend several lessons on one item if it proved interesting to the student. Or you may want to go on to a new object on which to focus questions:

knitting needles,

a spark plug,

a banana,

a potted plant,

a special food.

One tutor brought a bunch of grapes to use as a focal point for conversation and questions, ending the session by sharing the grapes with the student. The student had never seen or tasted grapes so there was a new taste experience as well as new vocabulary *(round, green, bunch, sweet, healthy, juicy, refreshing)*.

Ads from Newspapers

Provide ads clipped from newspapers so that you can discuss the product on sale, sales price, regular price, and how much savings there is. You might bring out the fact that often the merchandise on sale cannot be returned and that you must keep the sales slip to return merchandise. Role playing may be an interesting way to review this information with each of you alternately taking the role of the clerk and the customer.

Reading and Writing

Have your student read both silently and aloud. Ask questions to check comprehension and discuss together what your student has read. The stories can increase in difficulty as the student's language and reading skills develop.

Encourage your students to write lists, notes and answers to textbook questions as soon as possible. Again, assure them that you will give them the correct spelling and punctuation as needed.

Student's Country

Find out about holidays and particular customs in your student's country. These could be motivation for the student to stimulate conversation. Note vocabulary needs and the need for help in grammar as the student speaks.

News Broadcasts

Often a student can understand a face-to-face conversation with people who are familiar to him or her but has more difficulty with an unfamiliar voice, particularly if the student can't see the face of the speaker. It will help your student if you will tape news broadcasts which can be replayed several times as needed for understanding. Questions and discussions can follow.

American Holidays

Bring pictures or actual objects representative of traditional holidays — Halloween, Thanksgiving, Memorial Day, Remembrance Day, holidays that are very different from holidays in other countries. Get information on the origin of our holidays, and use pictures or objects such as a small pumpkin or a funny mask for Halloween, the U.S. flag or a picture of the men signing the Declaration of Independence for the Fourth of July, the Canadian flag for Dominion Day.

Action and Participation

It may provide a change of pace to go shopping with your student, or to visit a museum or a library. One tutor baked an apple pie with her student. The conversation and the new vocabulary that came out of this activity were excellent. Tape

recordings of some of these activities provide material for further lessons or role playing.

Dialogue

Don't forget dialogue. Instead of memorizing set-up dialogues, role-play situations which could relate to your student, e.g., pretending your student is seeking employment. You might act as the personnel officer and your student could be the applicant. On another occasion, pretend your student is going to a clinic. You could act as the receptionist with your student as the patient. When you are going through a role-playing activity, you want immediate response, so overlook many of the errors. Place more emphasis on comprehension of what is said and the student's ability to respond. You can tape such role-playing exercises so that your student can replay them or so you can review the tape for errors to help plan future lessons. Don't discourage your student from attempting conversation by focusing on errors. This may be so discouraging that he or she might find it easier not to try.

Grammar and Sentence Structure

Don't mention *grammar* specifically, but model correct structures having your student repeat and respond.

For example, to teach the present progressive tense verbs, you might bring objects for your student to use (pennies to count, cookies to eat, pins to put in a box) Ask your student what he is doing. If the student answers correctly:

"I'm counting pennies."

"I'm eating cookies."

Note that the present progressive tense is used correctly. However, if your student says:

"I count pennies."

you immediately model it correctly, having him repeat

T — "I'm counting pennies."

S — "I'm counting pennies."

If you're working on the past progressive verb, have your student do the same activities listed above (such as counting pennies). Ring a bell, clap your hands, or knock on the table to stop the activity. Ask your student what he was doing when you gave the signal to stop. Again, check in your note book if he had the past progressive tense under control by responding:

"I was counting pennies."

If the incorrect response was given, you model the correct response.

For the present, past, and future tenses, you could use a newspaper ad showing groceries and their prices. Say that you're going to plan tomorrow's shopping list. Ask your student to indicate what to buy by stating it in a sentence:

"Today we're buying tomatoes. The price is _____"

"Yesterday we bought bread and the price was _____"

"Tomorrow we'll buy lettuce. The price will be _____"

Continue with a practical, realistic list. Vary this with ads for clothing, hardware or drug items.

Working with the level III/IV student provides opportunity for each tutor to grow as well as to teach new ways to use English in daily living.

CHAPTER 13
Goals and Lesson Plans

Planning...Homework...Suggestions for Lesson Plans...Sample Lesson Plans for Level I/II Student ...Sample Lesson Plans for Level III/IV Student... Error Chart...Summary

Every student has a goal in mind when asking for help in conversational English. Sometimes these goals may take a long time to achieve. For example, a beginning conversational English student may wish to become a computer programmer, or to pass a GED (high school equivalency) exam. Or your student may want to gain confidence in listening or speaking skills in order to participate in a community meeting.

Whatever the goals, give encouragement by showing that progress is being made on short term objectives and long term goals. With only long term goals in mind, it is hard to develop lessons on a daily or weekly basis.

The first objective may be to be able to understand and respond to simple greetings in English. It may be learning enough "survival" vocabulary to do the daily shopping or to make an appointment with a doctor. These are here-and-now needs rather than projections into the far distant future. The short-term objectives may be revised as you progress together.

Planning

Planning for individual lessons is mainly your responsibility, but it should involve the student also. There may be immediate interests and needs which concern your student and these merit immediate attention, even though you will have to postpone the particular lesson you had planned for that day.

As you plan, keep in mind:

1. **Diagnosis.** Find out:
What your student knows now,
What individual weaknesses and strengths your student has,
What interests your student,
What your student wants to accomplish
(specific short-term objectives and long-term goals),
What your student's language needs are.
With these in mind, you can continue your planning.

2. **Teaching.** Use all the techniques.
Remember, if certain techniques work, they are right for your student. Use:
Listening, speaking, and comprehension drills,
Dialogue and role-playing,
Visual materials,
Texts and workbooks,
Reading and writing techniques

3. **Reinforcement.** Review and reteach by using approaches to build confidence and to strengthen your student's listening and speaking skills. Give suggestions for using

the newly-acquired skills outside of lesson time: TV, radio, tape-recorded English speech.

4. **Evaluation of lesson.** Ask both your student and yourself:
Have we done what we set out to do?
Is the student improving his/her listening and speaking skills?
Are weak spots being eliminated?
Are there new skills and ideas being gained by both student and tutor?
Is the student eager and contributing to the lesson or bored and discouraged?

The circle of planning becomes complete when you and the student go back to "diagnosis" and plan for the next lesson.

From diagnosis and a knowledge of the individual student's interests, lesson plans can be tailored to the student's individual learning style, using creative aproaches and as many materials as your ingenuity suggests.

It is difficult to plan a lesson until you have a specific person in mind, and know about that person's abilities and interests. When you are actually working with a student however, your lesson plans can be tailored to the needs of that specific person. Making realistic lesson plans is an important part of your teaching. Knowing what you are to do and how you will do it gives you confidence, eliminating that "What will I do next?" feeling. Your confidence communicates itself to your student. Planning allows you to be more flexible and more creative. It is always better to plan more than you can use rather than too little. Every lesson should be interesting and challenging but not frustrating.

To help in your lesson plans, keep a vocabulary check list. Words that need reinforcement will then be readily available.

Encourage your student to talk about things that are important in his/her everyday life. Keep a list of the student's expressed interests or needs so you include them in future lesson plans.

1. How to count money,
2. Terms used in shopping,
3. Conversational helps needed when talking on the telephone,
4. Conversational helps needed for a visit to the doctor or the clinic,
5. Vocabulary needed when traveling on a bus.
You might include questions people ask:
1. "**When** were you born?"..."did you get up?"..."did you leave for work?"..."did you come to America?"
2. "**Where** were you born?"..."did you come from?"..."do you live?"..."do you work?"
3. "**What** do you like to do for recreation?"..."do you

do at work?"..."is your Social Security number?"..."are you studying?"

4. "**Who or Whom** do you know in America?"..."do you work for?"..."do you work with?"..."can you call for help if it is needed?"

5. "**How** do you get to work?"..."do you spell your name?"..."did you come to America?"

6. "**Why** are you late for work?"..."do you need a car?"..."did your little boy miss school yesterday?"

An important source of topics for lessons as well as a check list of what your students might need to know is the "The Competency Based Mainstream English Language Training" (MELT) developed by the Office of Refugee Resettlement, US Department of Health and Human Service and presented in an abridged form in Appendix A.

While seeking to vary the lessons do not neglect repetition. The importance of repetition in the learning of a new language cannot be overstressed. The students need to hear and say words and phrases many times before they can be used automatically in actual situations. New vocabulary and structure should be repeated as often as possible after they are first taught.

Integrate new material immediately and begin to expand its context. For example, if you are teaching or reviewing the numbers in English, your student can progress from simple arithmetic to reading prices, telling time, and then giving change in American money. Help your student realize that what is being learned has many practical applications. Using the material in many different ways gives you an opportunity for repetition and review.

One of your long-range goals is to get your student to think in English. Personal involvement in the activities of the lesson helps. Involvement can be as simple as following directions, or it can be more complex, such as adding a sentence to a story you have started. In such a joint story-telling activity, you and your student can alternate giving sentences in the story. Hopefully this can be done rapidly so there's little delay and no time for translation from the native language to English. The object is to get the student to think fast in English, so don't stop to correct errors. Make notes on errors for later study.

Knowing techniques and drills thoroughly, a creative tutor can adapt to an individual student. It is helpful to use a textbook or two as road maps or guides to sequential learning. If a text seems rigid, use only what is helpful to you and make use of other books. The use of textbooks will give continuity to your lessons.

Many textbooks have simple placement tests which you may wish to use. Start your lessons at the point where your student falters or shows no understanding. A student may have a fairly good vocabulary, and may understand singular and plural, negatives and questions, and present tense. However, when it comes to past tense there are problems. Review quickly the earlier lessons in that text and concentrate on the more advanced lessons. Don't be misled into thinking your student understands because of a nod of the head. This is often a polite way to acknowledge your student's appreciation for what you are doing and to assure you of a continuing effort to comply with your wishes.

You are putting much effort into teaching your student all the skills involved in listening and speaking, but be sure you have time for fun. Games can provide practice in needed vocabulary or drills. To read something aloud that is of interest to the student can lend variety and can give examples of language which is well used. Your student will have practiced listening and your questions about the reading can provide a stimulus for independent speaking.

It is suggested that you use a spiral or loose-leaf notebook, putting specific things to be done on the left page, using the right page for your own comments. Or you can simply draw a line down the center of a page, using the left half for your lesson plans, the right half for your comments. These lesson plans can be very complete with much detail, or can be a simple outline. Use the one with which you're most comfortable.

You will save yourself a great deal of time and you will do much better job if you jot down your next lesson plan immediately after each lesson while the completed lesson is fresh in your mind. With your materials at hand, you can plan quickly and easily. If you need additional new materials, write a note to yourself and attend to it as soon as possible. The habit of writing up the next lesson immediately really pays dividends.

Begin your lesson with a short review of some material already learned. This is important for reinforcement, but it also allows the student to begin on material with which there is certain success, thus building confidence. However, bring in new material early in the lesson while the student is fresh.

Daily lesson plans will be as different as individual student's needs, abilities, and interests. This calls for sensitivity to the needs of the student and creativity in meeting those needs. However, consider the following list and include relevant items in most lesson plans.

You may want to refer to the MELT list or to the sequence of skills "A Check List" in the Appendixes for ideas about lesson content.

Homework

Language skills must be exercised to be acquired and maintained. No one learns a language without practice and it is the student who must provide the practice. False hopes are raised and time is wasted for both tutor and student to imply that a new language can be learned during the lesson time alone.

There must be daily practice on the part of the student. The effort of the student should match the efforts of the tutor who prepares carefully and is conscientious about instruction.

How can a beginning student practice listening and speaking skills without the tutor present?

1. Encourage your student to listen to spoken English — on TV, radio, in groups, in the family — even if it is not fully understood. To become surrounded by a new language helps one get the "feel" for its rhythm.

2. If your student has a tape recorder, record drills to be practiced or stories to be heard, suggesting he listen at his/her leisure.

3. Give your student an envelope, folder, or notebook for study materials. The student can repeat some of the class

activities alone or get an English-speaking friend or member of the family to help. The folder might include:

colored slips of paper,

numbers on 3 by 5 cards,

stick figure cards,

pictures.

4. Assign a simple task to perform, e.g. asking in English for the time, or to say an address or an English name written on a piece of paper.

Homework for the Level III/IV or more advanced student can include:

1. Participation in English-speaking groups, urging the student to speak, even though hesitantly and with an accent,

2. Assignment of listening to a specific TV or radio broadcast, knowing the tutor and the student will discuss it at the following lesson,

3. Reviewing alone (or with a friend) discussion about a picture which has been provided for the student,

4. Written dialogue that has been understood, to be practiced orally,

5. Taped sentences to be repeated,

6. Taped story read to the student at the lesson and reviewed at home,

7. A special task to perform, e.g. call long distance information for a certain number; ask someone in a store or on the street where such and such a street is; getting directions.

Some students are hesitant or neglectful about working at home. Make homework easier by giving much praise for improvement.

SUGGESTIONS FOR LESSON PLANS

Student's Name_____ Time_____ Date____

Levels I and II

1. Greeting.

2. Listening comprehension.

   (1) Commands — Directions: stand up, sit down, etc.

   (2) Colored paper exercises.

3. Vocabulary, using:

   (1) Substitution drill and response drill.

   (2) Objects.

   (3) Pictures without words.

4. Survival skills.

5. Textbooks, e.g. chapters on plurals, negatives, etc.

6. Simple dialogue.

7. Fun: pictures of your family, with simple descriptions; your student's country, giving the student something familiar to discuss, etc.

8. Tutor: Review this lesson, writing down your comments as a guide to planning the next lesson.

Levels III and IV

1. Conversation: Encourage your student to share recent experiences and to ask you questions. You can check pronunciation and structure in this free conversation time.

2. Review homework: Find out what was incompletely learned in order to give additional practice. Your student will welcome drill in difficult areas.

3. New material: Listening comprehension, vocabulary and speaking skills, reading and writing, using:

   (1) Pictures.

   (2) Textbooks.

   (3) Reading books.

   (4) Tape recorder.

   (5) Dialogue.

4. Relaxing activities for fun and reinforcement: games, reading a story together, or tutor reading a story which student can re-tell.

5. Homework assigned.

6. Tutor: Review this lesson, writing your comments as a guide to planning the next lesson.

Series of Three Sample Lessons for a Level I/II Student

LESSON 1

Materials to bring: Colored papers, Number flash cards, Calendar, Text, Pictures of tutor's family, Paper, Pen

1. Greeting:
    T — Hello, my name is *tutor's name*.
      How are you today, *student's name*?
    S — Fine, thanks, and you?
    T — Just fine.
   Your student may just smile in response. If so, go on with the lesson, but remind yourself to work on simple greetings.

2. Listening Comprehension: With strips of red and blue colored paper:
   Gesture for the student to listen.
   Hold any paper, saying "a paper." Repeat this with each piece of paper.
   Hold a blue paper, saying "a blue paper."
   Hold a red paper, saying " a red paper."
   (continuing until you're sure the student understands).
   Then pick up a blue (red) paper as you say:
   "I pick up a blue (red) paper."
   Put it on the table as you say:
   "I put a blue (red) paper on the table."
   Motion to the student as you say:
   "Pick up a blue (red) paper."
   "Put a blue (red) paper on the table."
   Repeat as many times as necessary for the student to demonstrate that he/she understands.

3. Speaking:
   Repeat the listening skills but gesture for the student to repeat — "a blue paper" - "a red paper" — etc.

4. Writing: Alphabet
   If a student does not read or write in the Roman alphabet you may suggest he/she practice writing (manuscript) the letters of the alphabet — repeating the names as you, and the student write.

5. Vocabulary:
   With flashcards, review orally, in order and randomly, numbers 1-10. With a calendar, review orally the first six months of the year. Substitution drill: (use articles in the room) - point to the table - point to the chair - point to the book - point to the pen. Repeat as many times as needed, adding as many objects as the student can handle. If the student demonstrates understanding, gesture for him/her to repeat, and have the student orally give you the same directions.

6. Textbooks or Worksheets:
   Reading and writing work to practice names of the months and numbers.

7. Conversation:
   With pictures of the tutor's family, tutor describes his/her family — how many brothers, sisters, children, sons, daughters he/she has. Tutor asks student simple questions, not expecting complete sentence answers: How many _____ do you have?
   Are they here (in U.S.) or in *(student's country)*?

8. Homework:
   Give student color papers to practice speaking. Ask student to bring in pictures of his/her family. For review of time, give the student a paper with the words learned in the lesson, written in manuscript. He/she can practice reading and writing them. Have the student write the letters of the alphabet in manuscript.

LESSON 2

Materials to bring: Colored papers, Number flash cards, Calendar, Text, Picture's of tutor's family, Paper, pen.

1. Greeting:
   Review as in Lesson 1, but omit "My name is ..."

2. Listening Comprehension: With strips of colored paper:
   Review Lesson 1 vocabulary and use of papers. Add appropriate demonstrations with paper as you say: "Give me a blue (red) paper." "Point to a blue (red) paper." Add "black paper," "yellow paper," fitting these new words into directions already learned.

3. Speaking:
   Have student repeat words already understood.

4. Writing: Alphabet
   Review writing letters of the alphabet, saying names.

5. Vocabulary:
   With flash cards, review numbers 1-10 and add more numbers (up to 15 or more if the student can handle them). With calendar, review orally the first 6 months of year, adding more months depending on the student's ability. Substitution drill —
   - Review Lesson 1, and add more articles
   - Add a new direction — "Touch" or "Pick up"

6. Textbooks or Worksheets:
   Reading and writing to practice numbers and months.

7. Conversation:
   Discuss student's family members as well as review tutor's family members.

8. Homework:
   Additional colored paper for practice. Additional words learned in vocabulary drills. Write letters of alphabet in manuscript. Textbook/Worksheets to practice numbers.

LESSON 3

Materials to bring: same as Lesson 1 and 2, American Flag, Birthday card.

1. Greeting:
   Review

2. Listening Comprehension: (colored paper)
   Review Lesson 1 and 2 — vocabulary and use of paper. Add appropriate demonstration with papers as you say "touch, it, him, her, one, two, three."

3. Speaking: (colored paper)
   Have student repeat words in listening skills and demonstrate understanding.

4. Writing:
   Write name, address, telephone number. Fill out simple form using the above.

5. Vocabulary:
   Review numbers 1-15 and add more.
   Calendar — review months of year.
   Calendar — teach names of days of week.
   Substitution drill:
      Review Lessons 1,2 and add more articles and new directions:
      "Put the book on the table."
      "Put the pen on the book."

6. Textbooks/Worksheets:
   Reading and Writing to practice numbers, months, days of week.

7. Discuss American holidays:
   Fourth of July
   Birthdays

8. Dialogues:
   T — "My birthday is (date) ."
        "When is your birthday?"
   S — "My birthday is (date) ."
   T — "I was born in America."
        "Where were you born?"
   S — "I was born in (country) ."

9. Homework:
   Same as 1.
   Same as 2.
   Write name, address, telephone number.
   Textbook/worksheets to practice numbers, months, days of week.

Series of Three Sample Lessons for a Level III/IV Student

LESSON 1

Materials to bring: apartment/floor plans, ads for apartment from newspaper, text.

1. Conversation:
   > Practice/discussion with simple past tense of verb -
   > "What did you do over the weekend?"
   > "Did you have a good weekend?"
   > "Where did you go?"
   > etc.

   Student then asks tutor similar questions, using simple past tense.

2. Review Homework

3. New Material:
   > Tutor has floor plan of his/her house or apartment.
   > Tutor describes house/apartment to student.
   > Student asks tutor questions:
   > "How many rooms...?"
   > "Where is the...?"
   > etc.

   Student draws floor plan of his/her apartment or house and describes it to the tutor. Tutor then asks student numerous questions.

   Discussions questions:
   > Do you have any problems in your house/apartment?
   > Practice answers which describe the problems clearly and accurately (don't work on solving the problems now).

   Dialogue between two friends: (present, and practice orally with picture cues)
   > A: Hi, how are you?
   > B: Not so good. I'm looking for a new apartment.
   > A: Why?
   > B: Mine is becoming a condominium.
   > A: What kind of apartment are you looking for?
   > B: A 2-bedroom apartment with heat included and a modern kitchen.

   Vocabulary Practice:
   > With flashcards, abbreviations often found in ads for apartments (apt., util.,furn.,fm., mo., sm., BR).

   Reading Practice:
   > Textbooks or newspaper — reading ads for apartments.

4. Reinforcement Activity:
   > Tutor and student each draw plan for his/her "dream" house/apartment. They describe their own house/apartment and ask each other questions.

5. Homework:
   > Textbook pages to practice reading apartment ads.

LESSON 2
Materials to bring: Pictures of apartment problems, and text.

1. Conversation:

   Practice with simple past and past progressive verb tenses:
   "I was shopping yesterday when it began to rain."
   "What were you doing?"
   "I was working Monday at 3:00. What were you doing?"

2. Review Homework

3. New Material:

   Review house/apartment problems that student came up with during the last session—add in other problems that may arise: leaky faucet, broken window, broken light, broken lock, broken table/TV, clogged toilet, clogged drain, broken stove/refrigerator.
   With picture of each problem -
   T — What should I do if I have a leaky faucet?
   S — If you have a leaky faucet, you should call the landlord/plumber.
   Reverse role — student cuing with picture and asking questions. Tutor responding.
   Reading practice/discussion -
   Dialogues or reading which go into more detail about one or two of the problems identified.

4. Reinforcement Activity:

   With picture of very dilapidated house (Eng. for Adult Comp., Book 2, p.109, Keltner and Bitterlin, Prentice-Hall, 1981), questions/answers and discussion about what happened (to practice simple simple past), and what should be done (to practice "should").

5. Homework:

   Textbook pages to practice "should," the simple past tense, the past continuous tense.

LESSON 3
Materials to bring: model or toy telephone, pen and paper,

1. Conversation:
    Tutor asks student to describe his/her home in his/her country.
    Tutor asks follow-up questions:
        "How was it different from where you are living now?"
        "What problems were there with the home in your country?"
        "How did these problems get taken care of?"

2. Review Homework

3. New Material:
    Review problems (generated last session) for which a tenant might call a landlord: leaky faucet, no heat, broken window. Dialogue (on telephone): cue visually with pictures or sketches:
    Landlord: Hello
    Tenant: Hello, Mr. Watson. This is Juan Diaz in apartment 3. I have a problem.
    Landlord: What's the matter?
    Tenant: There's a broken window in my kitchen.
    Landlord: Well, I'll try to get someone to fix it in a few days.
    Tenant: It's winter. It's too cold. It needs to be fixed right away.
    Landlord: I'll see what I can do.
    Practice dialogue (Student to memorize "tenant" lines)
    Discussion:
        "What should you do if the landlord isn't home"
            1. leave a message with whomever answers the phone.
            2. leave a note.
    Dialogue:
        Landlord's Daughter: Hello.
        Tenant: Hello, is Mr. Watson there?
        Landlord's Daughter: No, he isn't.
        Tenant: Could you give him a message?
        Landlord's Daughter: Sure.
        Tenant: This is Juan Diaz in apartment 3. There's a broken window in my kitchen. Please have him call me as soon as possible. My number is 865-5044.
    Writing Exercise:
        leaving a landlord a note

4. Homework:
    Textbook pages to practice dealing with apartment problems and the simple past tense..

Sample Lessons courtesy of Kathy Kuy, International Institute of Boston, Boston, Mass.; adapted by Ruth Colvin.

Error Chart

An "error chart" can be of real help in lesson planning. Rather than interrupting the lesson constantly to correct your student, jot down special problems to return to later. Sometimes you will want to correct your student immediately by modeling correctly, but often you may prefer to work on errors in future lessons.

ERROR CHART	
Errors	**Needs Help**
Says *shocks* for *socks*, *shun* for *sun*.	Work on /s/ sound.
Confuses *leg, lamp, lips, bedroom, bathroom*.	Work on words that sound alike (minimal pair exercises).

Summary

Your lesson plans are really good if they:

1. Are simple enough so that your student gains confidence with each lesson,

2. Give more repetition than you may think is necessary, thus making your student comfortable. It is better to overteach than to assume mastery too soon,

3. Reflect a feeling for your student's capabilities, needs, and interests,

4. Involve the teaching sequence of diagnosis, teaching, reinforcement, and evaluation.

5. Provide good materials for meeting your teaching goals,

6. Have continuity with the previous lesson,

7. Have ample variety to hold your student's interest.

You are a good tutor if you follow each lesson plan efficiently whenever you can, but are ready to adapt to special circumstance, to tailor all or part of a lesson, whenever an unexpected need or opportunity arises. Your lesson plans chart the course for teaching your student a new language. Make them carefully and use them efficiently.

CHAPTER 14
Small Group Meetings

Chain Drill...Conversation Starters...Vocabulary Games...Skits and Role Playing... Holiday Themes... Music...Have a Party.. A Stepping Off Point

After you have met with your student on a one-to-one basis for some time, you will probably look for ways to bring your student into experiences which will provide opportunities to interact with others. It may be possible to create or join a small group which can include several tutors and their students. The occasion may be a social event as well as a learning experience. These can be held monthly or four or five times a year. When your student has become accustomed to *your* voice, it would be helpful to hear and react to other voices. With you there as security, a group meeting can be an exciting introduction into American life.

It is also common for a tutor to begin instructing one student only to be asked by that student to teach another family member or a friend. You might find yourself tutoring a small group. The following are suggestions for adapting some of the techniques already given to a small group.

Chain Drill

A chain drill is a good introduction to a group, easy yet informative. Have the participants (both tutors and students) sit in a close circle. Start by saying:

"My name is _____ ."

Turn to the neighbor at your right and say:

"What's your name?"

That person responds with his or her name and asks the same question of the next person. This continues around the group.

The repetition is simple enough so that even the shy, beginning level student can participate and gain confidence. The chain drill can be expanded to other statements and questions that are appropriate for social settings. Always give your answer first as a model and then ask the question:

"I'm from New York State.

Where are you from?"

"I'm from Puerto Rico.

Where are you from?"

You might have a globe or a large map available and each person, both tutor and student, could point to the area from which he or she came. If one student is unfamiliar with a globe, let the other students help find his country.

You can add many questions, each time varying the chain drill a bit:

"I've been in Middletown thirty years.

How long have you been in Middletown?"

"I drove my car to the party.

How did you get here?"

"I have two children.

Do you have children?"

"I'm interested in golf and skiing.

What are you interested in?"

"I took a walk last night.

What did you do last night?"

This chain drill is fun and relaxing, and it gives good practice in listening and speaking skills.

Other Conversation Games

A good conversation game is "Twenty Questions." One person mentally picks out an object in the room or a well-known place or famous person. The others take turns asking questions that can be answered by "yes" or "no", trying to identify the object, place, or person. The person who identifies the answer correctly gets the opportunity to choose another object, place, or person.

Another chain drill activity is for the students to make up a narrative based on a picture. Each student adds *one phrase* to the story and must repeat all of the preceding phrases. For example:

T — "When Maria first came to America, she..."

lst Student — "...When Maria first came to America, she didn't have a friend."

2nd student — "...When Maria first came to America, she didn't have a friend or a teacher."

As each student adds a phrase the tutor determines if the word fits in grammatically and logically, remodeling it if necessary.

Conversation Starters

Free and easy conversation that is interesting and informative is what you strive for in these small conversational English groups. If you'll stop, look and listen to your own small social groups, you'll often note there are some individuals who dominate the group (the talkers) and others who sit back quietly (the listeners). This is natural in most social groups. A sensitive coordinator *can* soften the dominating individuals, bringing out the more shy persons so that they interact and both benefit by speaking and understanding English. Individuals within a small group *can* be encouraged to become both talkers and listeners. This is the responsibility of the coordinator and can be done through games as well as directed conversation.

It is helpful to have some plans made, some "conversation starters" in mind. If the students in a particular group are fairly basic, more structured activities are called for. But if the students are more advanced, you can plant the seeds by using tried conversation starters and they'll often continue on their own.

Vocabulary Games

Place some special object on the table. This object could be something from another country or something very familiar. Whatever it is, it's the focus of conversation. Have a variety of questions ready, soliciting discussion in English:

"What is this?"
"What's it made of?"
"What's it used for?"
"Where do you think it was made?"
"Do you have one?"
"Would you like one?"

If you are melding several groups, different tutors and students could supply these objects, giving each tutor/student team an opportunity to be the leaders. In an existing group, ask each student to bring in a object to use.

One activity that helps build vocabulary, especially for beginning students, is "I bought..." The tutor puts 12-15 articles on the table. I suggest they be related articles. e.g. kitchen articles such as napkins, matches, spatula, salt and pepper shakers, or toilet articles such as toothbrush, toothpaste, razor, tweezers. A tutor starts by saying:
"I went to the store and I bought napkins."
Each person takes his turn, adding one more article.
"I went to the store and I bought napkins, and matches."
"I went to the store and I bought napkins, and matches, and a spatula, ..."

After each person has had a chance to add to the list, give each student a *written* list of the words. Read them together and suggest that each student re-read them at home to the family when telling about the games at the party.

At one meeting, a Greek student had made spanakopita. Everyone enjoyed it so much and wanted to know how she made it. We adapted the "I bought" game by saying:
"Maria made spanakopita. She used flour."
"Maria made spanakopita. She used flour and water."
We included these ingredients: feta cheese, spinach, eggs, pepper, onions, and butter. There's repetition. Each student understands the vocabulary and says the words, and it's reinforced by reading. It's fun and yet a learning experience.

Be alert to ways you can capture new words from the students' conversations, explaining them and then letting the students carry the ideas further. We were discussing how individuals felt when they first came to America. Mary from Zaire in Central Africa had never seen snow or felt such cold when she arrived in Syracuse in mid-winter. In her limited English, Mary explained that she was confined to her small apartment. She said she was in a ...She groped for the right word. With gestures she made bars at the windows. We understood. "Prison." That opened the conversation to more vocabulary: *prisoner, thieves, vandals, judge, lawyer, fine* and *speeding*. More interesting anecdotes followed as each told of personal experiences.

"Show and Tell" gives individual students an opportunity to share. One student showed colored slides of her country, forgetting her embarrassment at her poor English in her enthusiasm of sharing her country with us. Another brought objects from her country, describing them and telling their use. Putting one student in the limelight each session brought pride and confidence to that student.

As you try to lead all students into the conversation, it's amazing how one thing leads right into another. We were enjoying strawberry shortcake. I said we really could **brag** about Alicia's strawberry shortcake. I saw eyebrows rise as I said *brag*. No one knew that word. I explained, giving examples and then each one was to *brag* about someone or something. It was revealing to hear students *brag* about their husband's work, their children's activities, their own cooking, their achievements at the university — being modest, yet proud.

Use pictures. At one time, four individual pictures from a series of pictures were passed out, with instructions to put them in order. After a little discussion among themselves, the students did get them in order. Then individuals described each picture as they entered into the project, with more and more words tumbling out.

Pictures can be the center around which conversation can be set. A picture of families at an American picnic brought excited conversation of similar outings in other countries, leading to talk of weather, food, games and activities.

There are hidden talents in every group. One man was a baker and gave a baking lesson when the meeting was in his home. Another woman showed how to quilt a small pillow. Another planted a miniature garden. As they worked, they talked. That's conversational English.

Skits and Role-Playing

Many of us are "hams". Try a little skit. You might write a short skit yourself. Or, there are several books available with two-three page stories, specifically geared to conversational English students, stressing specific skills. Make a copy of those few pages of the skit for each character, but *before* you give them these printed copies, read aloud the entire play or skit, acting it out yourself. They have *listened* first and understood. Then have them *read* the parts if their reading skills are up to it, or have them role play in keeping with what you have written for them.

Our first skit was "Fly Soup", (Hines, 1980) a two-page skit about a man in a restaurant who insisted that there was a fly in his soup. "Yes, there is." "No, there isn't." with a surprise ending when it was found that the man had a box of flies in his pocket, obviously getting free meals by dropping them into the food served. The students loved it, getting more dramatic each time they re-read the skit. Taping the third rehearsal gave them an opportunity to hear themselves and to laugh again. They didn't realize they were "arguing", expressing curiosity, using the present tense of "to be" with "this" and "that"— the objectives of the drama.

Or you can suggest a possible real life situation and have the students take different parts, role-playing. One group of young mothers was concerned about visiting the doctor with their children. We enacted a pretend visit to the doctor, including making an appointment, arriving and talking to the nurse, asking questions of the doctor, and reprimanding the children when necessary. This activity made the mothers feel more comfortable going into a real-life situation.

Because the conversational English small groups are similar to a class-room situation, check out the ideas given to class-room teachers in the many new books coming out. Adapt them and all will have fun as you learn together.

Holiday Themes

You could make an up-coming holiday the theme of a small group meeting, having appropriate objects, pictures, decorations, and possible songs.
Consider:

New Year's Eve,	Fourth of July,
Lincoln's Birthday,	Halloween,
Easter,	Thanksgiving,
Remembrance Day,	Hannukah,
Dominion Day,	Christmas,
St. Jean Baptiste Day,	Boxing Day,
Victoria Day,	Veterans' Day.

And don't forget to have your students share with the group *their* special holidays. We were discussing Memorial Day, honoring America's war veterans, which reminded the women from Japan of a Buddhist holiday. They said they would go to the cemetery to honor and show respect to their dead relatives — and celebrate by having a picnic afterwards.

In some Indo-Chinese countries birthdays are not celebrated and our birthday festivities are strange and new to them. Celebrating and explaining a birthday party could open up a new American tradition to many.

Music

Music is a wonderful bond between people. You might have a record or tape of a well-known American song, such as "Yankee Doodle", "Jingle Bells", "America the Beautiful", or "This Land is Your Land". If the tutors involved know your plans, they can teach their students the words and everyone can sing together the day of the party. There are excellent books devoted to using music to teach English, making it fun for all involved.

Have a Party

If you and some fellow tutors are not teaching in small groups but would like to initiate an opportunity for your students to have some of the advantages of group interaction while still maintaining the security of the one-to-one situation, you could begin with a party.

It is helpful if all the tutors involved are told what will be done at the "coffee" or party so that they can prepare the students. It is not wise to have students from only one country or to have only one language represented. Having English as the only language common to all makes it necessary for the students to speak English.

As there are advantages to meeting one-to-one, there are also advantages to meeting in small groups. One goal is to help students become comfortable with English as the only language used in conversation. With the tutor there for support, each student can start reaching out, looking forward to eventually being able to attend social functions alone in this country.

Foreign-born students are often isolated and these small group meetings give opportunities for new friendships as well as a way to learn of other cultures. Often a real sense of belonging is developed, strengthening a feeling of being accepted. But don't overlook your real purpose in working with your conversational English students - their needs and desire to understand and speak English better.

Students and tutors can practice traditional greetings and reponses so that they feel at ease at the gathering. Coffee, tea, or other refreshments can be provided (perhaps by the students) to make it more of a party. It is helpful to have one person act as coordinator or facilitator, leading the group discussion. Keep the activities simple and be sure that all the students can participate. Be sensitive to the students' abilities to understand and speak English, and their interest in the varied activities.

Pot-luck dinners with conversational English students are wonderful. Ask the student to prepare some food native to their countries. The resulting feelings of friendship and sharing are tremendous language generators.

A Stepping off Point

Your meetings can be as varied as the people involved, centering discussions in English on a variety of subjects:
> favorite foods,
> gardening,
> buying a car,
> family activities,
> weather in your particular area,
> sports,
> nature study,
> travel maps.

Small group meetings may give your student enough confidence to attend a church or community meeting. They can encourage greater social interaction and they can be lots of fun. These group activities may be just what is needed to initiate or continue an interest in adult education classes.

CHAPTER 15

Tutor Competency Evaluation

**Attitudes...Diagnosing Your Student...Teaching Skills...General Information...
Case Histories**

Attitudes

Before you begin to instruct a student, you should evaluate your attitudes, as well as the skills you will need to provide successful instruction in teaching conversational English:

1. Am I free of critical attitudes toward those who cannot speak, understand, read and write English? My answer requires absolute honesty in examining my own attitudes toward those who are from other countries.

2. Am I willing to be patient with small gains and with the possibility of a long period of instruction?

3. Am I enthusiastic enough in my instruction to *provide genuine encouragement* so that my student can experience a feeling of achievement with the many small successes needed before any long-term goals can be achieved? (See Pages 10-12).

Diagnosing Your Student

1. When will I test my student? (see page 15).
2. How will I find out if a prospective student:
   a. can *understand* English at all?
   b. can *speak* English at all?
   c. is at a more advanced level of conversational English? (see page 15)
   d. can read/write in his/her native language? In English? (see page 16)

Teaching Skills

1. What two language skills am I most concerned about when teaching English as a second language?
Reinforced by what two other skills? (see page 4)
2. If my student tests at Level I, in what area would I concentrate my tutoring?
   a. at Level II?
   b. at Level III?
   c. at Level IV? (see page 15)
3. What are some practical ways to practice listening comprehension? (see pages 29, 30)
4. Describe at least three survival skills which could be taught: (see pages 21-24)
5. What are several tools I can use to communicate as I teach my student? (see pages 26, 41-43)
6. Give an example of each of the following techniques:
   a. Simple substitution drill
   b. Complex substitution drill
   c. Response drill
   d. Transformation drills:

Positive to negative
Statement to question
   e. Backward buildup
   f. Two creative drills (see pages 37, 38)
7. Write a simple dialogue. Describe the steps necessary to teach this dialogue. (see page 35-37)
8. List several things that should be included in each lesson plan. (see page 60)

General Information

1. Am I willing to get more information about my student's country and culture? (see page 13)
2. If my student wants to become a citizen, where will I go for useful information? (see pages 86, 87)

Case Histories

With the following five student case histories, how would you answer these questions?
1. What supplies would you have with you?
2. How would you find the conversational and comprehension level of your student?
3. What techniques would you use in teaching?
4. From what you know about this individual, what specific materials and texts would you use?
5. Can you think of other ways to help?
In these case histories, the results of testing are given to you. In reality, such testing may be your responsibility. If so, testing should be done as soon as possible, after the student has been assigned.
1. **Francisco is a 19-year old Sicilian man** who has had six years of schooling in his native land. He has been in the United States for one year and lives with his elderly father in an apartment house, where Francisco is the maintenance man. He also works two hours a day as a bagger in a supermarket. His ambition is to join the Air Force where he can be with the planes he loves, but he knows that he must have more English than the few conventional phrases he now speaks. His working schedule is such that it is impossible for him to attend Adult Education classes. He tries to help himself by listening to radio newscasts, but his small knowledge of English hinders his understanding of their content. He enjoys biking and playing bocce ball. He tests at Level I.
2. **Muy is a Vietnamese mother**, 30 years old, who has been in this province three months. She has a five-year-old daughter and a six-year-old son, and is expecting another child in six months. Muy speaks fluent French and reads

and writes in her own language, but her English is halting and difficult to understand because of her intonation difficulty and sparse vocabulary. She faces two problems in communication: her inability to converse with her children's teachers and her need to discuss her pregnancy with an English-speaking doctor. She tests at Level II.

3. **Danno is a 15-year-old boy** from Puerto Vallarta, Mexico. He has lived in this country about eleven months and is in the eighth grade. Because of his language difficulty (he speaks only "street" English and not much of that), he is in danger of dropping out of school. He wants to stay in school because he dreams of being on the track team, but he's falling behind in all of his subjects except math. His native-born schoolmates harass him because of his school performance and also because he's Mexican. Consequently, he's become shy and somewhat surly. He has no special hobbies and spends his time on the streets with his Mexican friends, thinking up ways to get even with the Anglos. He tests at Level III.

4. **Rosa is a widow born 53 years ago** in a village in Italy and has recently been brought to the United States by her eldest son. Rosa is unable to read and write in her native language and had no schooling in her little village. She is most unhappy because she can converse only with her son since his American wife and children know only a few words of Italian. Rosa feels very much a displaced person, missing the community life of the village, her neighbors, and her important position as the local mid-wife. She does not understand the customs and life style of her American family and her son is often too busy to answer her questions. Crocheting and Sunday Mass (alas, in English, also!) are her only pleasures. She wants to speak and be understood — to ask questions and understand the answers. She tests at Level I.

5. **Bernard is a 24-year-old Russian Jew** who came to this country from Kiev three months ago. He speaks and reads Russian and Hebrew and has a reading knowledge of English. He is attending Adult Education classes but needs special tutoring if he is to attain his goal — to be accepted at the University in the fall. His English is stilted and hesitant; he begs people to slow down in speaking to him, and he's confused by local idioms. He tends to "think" in Russian and "translate" into English. He tests at Level IV.

It's exciting to watch your student grow in language skills and to learn as you teach. You should become confident in your ability as a tutor as you use the techniques you have been taught in this book. You may find a whole new world opening up. The experience will surely prove to be a rich one for both you and your student.

What better way to pay homage to our own immigrant forefathers (or grandfathers, or fathers) than to reach out a helping hand to the newcomers who have come to live in America — to share our language with a stranger so that he can live more meaningfully in our corner of the globe? When we open channels of communication with a person of a different culture, our insights are sharpened and we can truly conceive of the peoples of the world as brothers.

Both student and tutor have something to give and something to gain. The tutor gives new skills in English and the student gives the gift of insight into another culture. May the exchange prove worth the effort to both of you!

RECOMMENDED READING

Basic Texts

Boggs, Ralph S. and Dixon, Robert J.
1980 **English Step-by-Step With Pictures.** New York: Regents Publishing Company, Inc.

Castro, Oscar
1980 **In Touch.** New York: Longman, Inc.

Ferreira, Linda M.
1985 **Express English: Beginnings 1.** Rowley, MA.: Newbury House Publishers.

Foley, Barbara and Pomann, Howard
1981 **Lifelines. (Books 1-3).** New York: Regents Publishing Company, Inc.

Kellner, Autumn
1983 **Basic English for Adult Competency.** Englewood Cliffs, NJ.: Prentice Hall

Molinsky, Steven
1980 **Side by Side.** Englewood Cliffs, NJ.: Prentice Hall.

Molinsky, Steven and Bliss, Bill
1984 **Line by Line.** Englewood Cliffs, NJ.: Prentice Hall

O'Neil, Robert, Kingsbury, Roy, et al.
1978 **American Kernel Lessons** (Intermediate). New York: Longman, Inc.

Quan and Schurer
1980 **Everyday English** (4 books). Hayward, CA.: Alemany Press.

Zern, Guenther
1985 **Images (1 and 2). English for Beginners.** Reading, MA.: Addison Wesley.

Citizenship

Wiener, Solomon
1982 **Questions and Answers on American Citizenship** (Revised) New York: Regents Publishing Co.

Composition

Abdulaziz, Helen and Shenkarow, Helen
1985 **Write it Right: Beginning Handwriting and Composition Skills for Students of ESL.** Englewood Cliffs, NJ.: Prentice Hall.

Baskoff, Florence
1971 **American English Guided Composition.** Chicago: Rand McNally.

Blanton, Linda L.
1982 **Elementary Composition Practice Book.** (2 books). Rowley, MA.: Newbury House.

Brooks and Witherow
1984 **10 Steps:** Controlled composition for beginning and intermediate students. Hayward, CA.: Alemany Press.

Conversation/Vocabulary

Byrd, Donald and Clemete-Cabetas, Isis
1980 **React/Interact.** New York: Regents Publishing Company.

Carver, Tina and Fotinas, Sandra
1977 **A Conversation Book: English in Everyday Life.** Englewood Cliffs, NJ.: Prentice-Hall.

Dobson, Julia and Sedwick, Frank
1981 **Conversation in English: Points of Departure.** Hollywood, FL: Atlantis Publishers.

Dobson, Julia and Hawkins, Gerald
1978 **Conversation in English: Professional Careers.** Hollywood, FL: Atlantis Publishers.

Gilbert, Doris Wilcos
1978 **Breaking the Sound Barrier.** Englewood Cliffs, NJ: Prentice Hall

Palmer, Rogers and Olsen
1985 **Back and Forth** (Pair Activities). Hayward, CA.: Alamany Press.

Paulston, Christine Bratt
1975 **Developing Communicative Competence: Roleplays.** Pittsburg, PA: University of Pittsburgh Press.

Pifer, George and Muton, Nancy
1977 **Points of View.** Rowley, MA.: Newbury House.

Yorkey, Richard
1985 **Talk-A-Tivities.** Reading, MA.: Addison Wesley.

Culture

Brigham Young University, Language and Research Center **Culturegrams.** Provo, UT.

Ford, Carol and Silverman, Ann
1981 **American Cultural Encounters.** Hayward, CA.: Alemany Press.

Messec, Jerry L. and Kranich, Roger E.
1982 **Life in the United States.** (Text and Student's Exercise Book. New York: Cambridge, The Adult Education Company.

Zanger, Virginia
1985 **Face to Face: A Cross-Cultural Workbook.** Rowley, MA.: Newbury House.

Dictionary

Parnell, E.C.
1978 **Oxford Picture Dictionary of American English.**: New York: Oxford University Press.

English Through Music

Graham, Carolyn
  1978 **Jazz Chants.** New York: Oxford University Press.
Kind, Ewe
  1980 **Tune in to English.** New York: Regents Publishing Company.

Grammar

Azar, Betty
  1981 **Understanding and Using English Grammar.** Englewood Cliffs, NJ.: Prentice Hall.
Dart, Allen Kent
  1978 **ESL Grammar Workbook.** Englewood Cliffs, NJ.: Prentice Hall
Dixson, Robert J.
  1978 **Essential Idioms in English** (Revised). New York: Regents Publishing Co. Inc.
Hook, J.N.
  1981 **Two Word Verbs in English.** New York: Harcourt Brace Jovanovich International.
Reeves, George
  1985 **The New Idioms in Action.** Rowley, MA.: Newbury House.

Pronunciation

Nilsen, Don. L. F., Nilsen, Aileen, P.
  1973 **Pronunciation Contrasts in English.** New York: Regents Publishing Co. Inc.
Tillet, Bruce and Buder, Mary N.
  1978 **Speaking Naturally.** New York: Cambridge University Press.
Traeger, Edith and Henderson, Sara C.
  1956 **Pronunciation Drills: the PD's.** Encino, CA.: English Language Services.

Readers

Clark, Raymond C.
  1985 **Potluck.** Brattleboro, VT.: Pro Lingua Associates.
Felder, Mira and Bromberg, Anna
  1980 **Light and Lively.** New York: Harcourt Brace, Jovanovich. Gonshack, Sol
  1976 **Little Stories for Big People.** New York: Regents Publishing Co. Inc.
Hines, Mary Elizabeth
  1973 **Skits in English.** New York: Regents Publishing Co. Inc.
Miller and Clark
  1984 **Smalltown Daily.** Brattleboro, VT.: Pro Lingua Associates.
Simmons, Judy
  1983 **A Light in the Dark.** New York: Cambridge, The Adult Education Company.

Reading Comprehension

Bodman, Jean and Lanzano, Michael
       No Hot Water Tonight. New York: Collier MacMillan.
Baudoin, Margaret, et al.
  1971 **Readers' Choice: A Reading Skills Textbook for Students of English as a Second Language.** Ann Arbor, MI: University of Michigan Press.
Lawson, V.K. et al
  1984 **Read All About It! Tutoring Adults with Daily Newspaper.** Syracuse, NY.: Literacy Volunteers of America, Inc.
Markstein, Linda and Hirasawo, Louise
  1974 **Developing Reading Skills** (Intermediate). Rowley, MA.: Newbury House.
Troyka, Lynn Q.
  1978 **Structured Reading.** Englewood Cliffs, NJ.: Prentice Hall.

Vocabulary Through Pictures

Boyd, John R., and Boyd, Mary Ann
  1982 **Alice Blows a Fuse: 50 Strip Stories in American English.** Englewood Cliffs, NJ.: Prentice Hall.
Moran, Patrick
  1984 **Lexicarry.** Brattleboro, VT.: Pro Lingua Associates.
  1984 **Picture It! Sequences for Conversation.** New York: Regents Publishing Company, Inc.

Instructor Reference

Clark, Raymond C.
  1980 **Language Teaching Techniques.** Brattleboro Vt.: Pro Lingua Associates.
Colvin, Ruth, and Root, Jane
  1984 **Tutor** (Revised). Syracuse, N.Y.: Literacy Volunteers of America, Inc.
  1982 **Read** (Revised). Syracuse, N.Y.: Literacy Volunteers of America, Inc.
Coye, Joy; Gonzalez, David R.; Santupietro, Kathy.
  1980 **English Second Language Oral Assessment** Syracuse, N.Y.: Literacy Volunteers of America.
Krashen, Stephen D.,and Terrell, Tracy D.
  1983 **The Natural Approach: Language Acquisition in the Classroom.** Hayward, CA.: Alemany Press.
MacDonald, Marion and Rogers-Gordon, Sue
  1982 **Action Plans.** Rowley, MA: Newbury House.
McMichael, Carolyn and Coor, William
  1983 **A Guide to Gestures in the ESL Classroom.** Denton, Texas: Texas University.

Tutor Resource - Lesson Plans

Graham, C. Ray, and Walsh, Mark M.
   n.d.   **Adult Education ESL Tutor's Guide.** Kingsville, Texas: Texas A&I University.

Humanistic Resources

Moskowitz, Gertrude
   1978   **Caring and Sharing in the Foreign Language Class.** Rowley, MA.: Newbury House Publishers.

BIBLIOGRAPHY OF BOOKS CITED

Allen, Dan, and Hall, Richard
1975 **New Lives in the New World.** New York: Mac-millan International.
Clark, Raymond C.
1980 **Language Teaching Techniques.** Brattleboro, VT.: Pro Lingua Associates.
Colvin, Ruth, and Root, Jane
1984 **Tutor** (Revised). Syracuse, N.Y.: Literacy Volunteers of America, Inc.
Coy, Joye Jenkins, and Gonzalez, David R
1980 **English Second Language Oral Assessment.** Syracuse, N.Y.: Literacy Volunteers of America, Inc.
Durant, Will
1954 **The Story of Civilization, Part 1, Our Oriental Heritage.** New York: Simon and Shuster.
Flavier, Juan
n.d. **Doctor of the Barrios.** Quezon City, Republic of the Philippines: New Day Publishers of the Christian Literature Society.
Gattegno, Caleb
1972 **The Silent Way: Foreign Languages in Schools.** New York: Educational Solutions, Inc.
Hall, Edward T
1966 **The Hidden Dimension.** New York: Doubleday & Company, Inc.
Hines, Mary Elizabeth
1980 **Skits in English.** New York: Regents Publishing Company, Inc.

Hormby, A.S.
1974 **Oxford Advanced Learners Dictionary of Current English.** New York: Oxford University Press.
Kuy, Kathy, and Thomas, Bob
1985 **Handbook for Volunteer ESL Literacy Teachers.** Boston: International Institute.
McMichael, Carolyn, Coor, Michael
1983 **A Guide to Gestures in the ESL Classroom.** Unpublished paper. TESOL, North Texas University in Denton.
Ossoff, Ellen E
The Picture File: Its Assembly and Use. Unpublished paper.
1976 **The Bilingual Dictionary as an Aid for Teaching ESL.** Unpublished paper.
Poczik, Robert
1974 **Teaching English as a Second Language: A Self-Instructional Course.** Albany, NY: New York State Education Department.
Schwan, Mary
1979 **Introduction to Teaching English as a Second Language to Adults.** Pampas Press.
Senior, Clarence
1965 **The Puerto Ricans-Strangers then Neighbors.** Anti-Defamation League of B'nai B'rith. Quadrangle Books, Inc.

Appendix A

The Competency Based Mainstream English Language Training (MELT)

(from the Office of Refugee Resettlement, U.S. Department of Health and Human Services, 330 C Street, S.W. Switzer Building, Washington, D.C. 20201)

Part I - Competencies Listed by Topic
From Lowest to Highest Levels of Difficulty

```
                        KEY

( ) — Language example for competency statement
[ ] — Language example that students are expected
to listen to and understand
(" ") — Language example that students are expected
to produce.
(CAPITALS) — Language example that students are
expected to read and understand.
```

BANKING
Endorse a check

Provide proper ID upon request to cash a check or money order ("Can I cash this check?")

Buy a money order ("A money order for $50.00, please.")

Write a check

Fill out a money order, including date, amount, name of addressee, own name and signature.

Fill out deposit/withdrawal slips.

Buy and fill out an international money order.

Fill out the required forms to open a checking or savings account with assistance.

Read a savings and checking account statement.

Fill out a loan application with assistance.

COMMUNITY SERVICES
Read emergency words (FIRE, POLICE, POISON).

Read, say and dial telephone numbers of emergency services (FIRE-991).

Spell name and address and report an emergency in the home by telephone in simple terms. (Help!; Police!)

Ask for stamps at a post office ("Two airmail stamps, please.")

Identify basic facilities, services and commonly seen community workers in the neighborhood/community ("Bank", "money", "teller", "Hospital", "sick", "doctor.")

Report an emergency in person. ("Help! Fire in Apartment 2A!")

Correctly address an envelope/package, including return address.

Provide upon request proof of address or other necessary information in order to obtain a library card [Can I see your driver's license?] ("Yes, here you are".)

Report location and problem in an emergency outside the home ("Help! There's a robbery at 10 Main Street!")

Ask and answer questions about the name of own or child's school, teacher, class, and time. [(Which school does your child go to?] "Lincoln School.")

Read and interpret common signs regarding hours in public areas (PARK CLOSED AT 6:00).

Fill out a change of address form, with assistance.

Ask simple questions to determine correct postage. ("How much is this letter by airmail?")

Write a note or call to explain an absence from school. ("I was absent yesterday because I went to the dentist.")

Respond to postal clerk's questions regarding custom forms and insurance forms for domestic and overseas packages. [(What's inside?] "Clothing." [("What's the value?"] ("25.00).

Respond to serious weather conditions based on a TV, radio, or telephone warning. ([There's a tornado watch until 10:00 tonight.])

Inquire about the availability of vocational training or adult basic education programs. ("Is there a welding class that I can take?")

Read and respond appropriately to written communications from child's school — shortened school day, vacation, parent-teacher meeting.

Read basic information on child's report card. (P = PASS, F = Fail.)

Ask for information about, and locate on a map, public recreational facilities and entertainment ("Where can I go fishing?")

Fill out postal forms, such as letter registration forms, without assistance.

Arrange day care or pre-school for own children ("I'd like to enroll my daughter in pre-school.")

Assist others in reporting an emergency with limited translation as necessary.

Obtain information about local public recreational facilities and entertainment from pre-recorded messages.

Ask about service provided by a public library ("Can I renew these books?"; "Can I borrow records?")

Read information about education, health, and other community services in a community newsletter.

Accompany and assist a person at a clinic or in an emergency room.

Report a suspected loss or theft. ("I didn't get my check in the mail. I think someone stole it.")

Get information from local media sources - newspaper, TV, and radio - on education, legal and health, and other community services - to obtain a fishing license, legal advice, etc. order merchandise by mail. Report problems about mail order merchandise by telephone or in a letter. ("I haven't received my order yet. It's two weeks late.")

EMPLOYMENT — FINDING A JOB

State previous occupation in simple terms ("Cook.")

State current job status. (["Do you have a job?"] ("No." or " Yes.")

State desire to work in simple terms. ("I want a job.")

State own job skills in simple terms. ("I can cook.")

Copy basic personal information on a simple job application form. (NAME, SOCIAL SECURITY NUMBER, AGE, ADDRESS)

Read HELP WANTED sign.

Identify some common entry-level jobs which can be held by those with limited English ability.

Respond to specific questions about previous work experience using short phrases, including occupation(s), length, and dates of employment [(What was your job?] "Cook." [How long?] "Ten years".)

Fill out a simple job application form, excluding previous or current occupation(s) and dates of employment.

Ask others to help in finding a job, e.g., from a sponsor,job developer, or friends. ("I need a job.")

Inquire about job openings and determine a time for an interview in person. ("Is there a job opening for a housekeeper?" [Yes.] "What time can I interview?" [Monday, at 9:00])

State own situation in regard to work shifts, starting date, specific hours, and payday. ("I can work 3 to ll.")

Answer basic direct questions about pay, work availability, and hours ([Is $4.00 an hour OK?"] "Yes." [When can you start?] "Tomorrow." [Can you work nights?] "Yes.")

Express concerns and fears about the job in simple terms. ("The job is dangerous.")

Read want ads and identify skills needed for a job.

Describe previous work experience, job skills, qualifications and training, including degrees of ability. ("I can fix trucks".; "I have a lot of experience.")

Read signs and notices posted at work-site, agency, etc. advertising positions available; ask for clarification (if necessary). Indicate several general types of entry-level in the U.S. and their respective duties, qualifications, and working hours. ("Factory work"; "sort parts"; "no experience required"; "full-time.")

Answer basic questions about educational background, including dates and location(s) (by country). ([What is your educational background?] "I finished high school in Iraq in 1970.")

State long-term goals ("I'd like to be a supervisor.")

Fill out a standard job application form; ask for assistance when needed.

Begin and end an interview appropriately; answer and ask questions and volunteer information, if necessary.

Find out about benefits for a new job. ("What kinds of benefits are available?")

State own ability related to work. ("I learn quickly.")

Respond appropriately to an employer's decision about a job, whether accepted or rejected. ([I'm sorry but the job is filled.] "Do you have any other openings?")

Make a follow-up call about a job application. ("Did the manager review my application?")

Use a telephone to inquire about advertised and unadvertised job openings for an interview. ("Do you have any job openings?" [Yes, we do]. ("What jobs are available?")

Discuss job advancement opportunities, requirements and procedures with supervisor or counselor. ("I'd like to apply for the position of supervisor. What are the procedures?")

Write a basic resume with assistance.

Write a cover letter and follow-up letter when applying for a job, with assistance.

EMPLOYMENT — ON THE JOB

Ask if a job was done correctly. ("OK"?)

Ask simple clarification questions about routine job tasks and instructions. ("Please repeat."; "Do this?")

Respond to simple direct questions about work progress and completion of tasks. ([Are you finished?] "No.")

Ask supervisor or co-worker for help. ("Can you help me?")

Sign name on time sheet.

Respond to simple oral warnings or basic commands about safety. [(Watch out!]

Read common warning or safety signs at the work site; (DANGER)

Read alpha-numeric codes. (AF 47)

Give simple excuses for lateness or absence in person. ("I was sick yesterday.")

State need for frequently used materials. ("I need boxes.")

Report work progress and completion of tasks. ("I'm finished.")

Find out about the location of common materials and facilities at the work site. ("Where is the supply room?")

Follow simple one-step oral instructions to begin and to perform a task which is demonstrated, including simple classroom instructions. [(Put these away.])

Ask for permission to leave work early or to be excused from work. ("Can I go home?")

Give simple excuses for lateness or absence on the telephone. ("My name's Tran. I'm sick today.")

Follow simple oral instructions which contain references to places or objects in the immediate work area. ([Get me the box over there.])

Modify a task based on changes in instructions. [(Wait! Don't use that!])

Ask/tell where a co-worker is ([Where's Tran?]) "He's in the cafeteria.")

Give simple one-step instructions to co-workers. ("Put the tools over there.")

Follow simple two-step directions on the job. ([Take this and put it on the shelf.])

Respond to supervisor's comments about quality of work on the job, including mistakes, working too slowly, and incomplete work. ("I'm sorry. I won't do it again.")

Give specific reasons for sickness, absence, or lateness. ("I had the flu. I had to go to the doctor.")

Report specific problems encountered in completing a task. ("I don't have any more paper.")

Read first name and department on employer name tags . (ROSE. DEPARTMENT 10.)

Respond to multiple-step oral instructions without visual references. ([Take the box in the hall to the mailroom and put it on the top shelf.])

Briefly explain a technique or the operation of a piece of basic equipment to a co-worker. May use gestures or a demonstration. ("You have to loosen the screw and raise it up.")

State intention to resign and give reasons for resigning from the job ("I'm going to quit my job in three weeks because I'm moving.")

Request a letter of reference. ("Could you write a reference letter for me?")

Report and describe the nature of problems on the job. ("The stairs are dangerous because they're wet.")

Read a simple work memo, asking for assistance if necessary.

Fill out accident report forms with assistance.

Teach a routine task to a co-worker using step-by-step verbal instructions and some demonstrations.

Read own employment reviews, including explanations of promotion or probation.

Read most simplified on-the-job audio-visual training materials for entry-level jobs.

Read and fill out health insurance forms with the use of bilingual reference materials.

Read basic non-technical personnel policies and benefit documents with assistance if needed.

Ask about regular paycheck deductions and question irregularities. ("Why is my FICA deduction more this month?")

Read written safety regulations and operating instructions for tools and equipment.

Explain a technique or the operation of a complicated machine such as a drill press.

Initiate and maintain conversations at the work site, such as the advantages or disadvantages of joining a union.

Write a short work memo.

HEALTH

State own general condition in simple terms. ("I'm tired.")

State need for medical help. ("Help. I'm sick.")

Read simple signs related to health care. (HOSPITAL, EMERGENCY, PHARMACY, DRUG STORE.

Identify major body parts. ("Arm"; "stomach"; "leg.")

State major illnesses or injuries. ("Sore throat"; "broken arm.")

Make a doctor's appointment in person, giving own name, address, and telephone number when asked.

Read time and date for a medical appointment from an appointment card. (THURSDAY, DECEMBER 26, AT 3:00).

State a need for an interpreter. ("I don't speak English. I speak Vietnamese.")

Follow simple instructions during a medical exam. ([Open your mouth; Take off your shirt. Take a deep breath.])

Ask for a familiar non-prescription medication at the drug store. ("I want a bottle of aspirin.")

State others' health problems in simple terms. ("His arm hurts.")

Determine and report body temperature as indicated by a thermometer. ("My temperature is 100.")

Ask for a patient's room number in a hospital. ("What is Sarem Nouan's room number?")

Identify oneself, one's appointment, and doctor's name, if applicable, upon arrival at the doctor's office. ("I'm Sarem Nouan. I have a 2:00 appointment." [Which doctor?] ("Dr. Smith.")

Ask about and follow simple instructions for using medicine ("How much?"; "How many?")

State symptoms associated with common illnesses. ("I have diarrhea.")

Read the generic names of common non-prescription medicines. (ASPIRIN, COUGH SYRUP)

Read and follow directions on medicine labels, including abbreviations. (TAKE 2 TSP. 3 TIMES A DAY.)

Ask for assistance in locating common non-prescription medicines. ("Where is the aspirin?")

Follow simple oral instructions about treatment.([Stay in bed. Take one pill every day.])

Locate facilities within a hospital by reading signs. (X-RAY, CAFETERIA).

Ask a doctor or nurse about own physical condition or treatment plan using simple language. ("What's the problem/matter? Can I go to work?")

Describe own emotional state and explain the reason for it. ("I am sad because I think about my family in Cambodia.")

Make a doctor's appointment on the telephone, giving name address, telephone number, and the nature of the problem, and request a convenient day and time — after school or work hours.

Change or cancel a doctor's appointment in person. ("I'd like to cancel my appointment on March 10.")

Report lateness for a medical appointment by telephone. ("I'm going to be 30 minutes late. Is that OK?")

State results of a visit to a doctor/clinic/hospital to employer or teacher. ("The doctor says I can come back to work.")

Fill out a simple insurance form with assistance.

Respond to simple questions about physical disability ([Do you have any health problems?] "I have allergies.")

Telephone or write a simple note to school/work explaining own or child's absence due to illness. ("My daughter was absent yesterday because she had the flu.")

Read warnings, storage directions, and emergency instructions (REFRIGERATE AFTER OPENING, KEEP OUT OF THE REACH OF CHILDREN).

Describe general medical history orally, including names of major illnesses. ("I had hepatitis in 1980.")

Respond to questions about means of payment. ([Do you have Medicaid or personal insurance?] "Medicaid.")

Fill out a simple medical history form with assistance. May use bilingual materials if needed.

Explain own and others' health problems in detail. ("My back hurts when I lift heavy objects.")

Offer advice for health problems. ("You've been sick for a long time. Why don't you see a doctor?")

Fill out a standard medical history form with assistance.

Read about and describe some possible side effects of medication. (DROWSINESS MAY RESULT)

Read routine clinic notice/reminders — hours, payment requirements, policies concerning cancelled appointments.

Read immunization requirements for school and work.

HOUSING

Identify common household furniture/rooms. ("Kitchen; bathroom.")

Read exit route signs in housing. (EXIT, FIRE ESCAPE)

Identify basic types of available housing ("Apartment; house.")

Report basic household problems and request repairs in simple terms. ("The toilet is leaking. Please fix it.")

Report basic household emergencies by telephone — fire, break-ins, etc.; give and spell name, address, and give telephone number when asked.

Answer simple questions about basic housing needs. ([What kind of an apartment are you looking for?] ("I need three bedrooms.")

Ask how much the rent is. ("How much is the rent?")

Read common housing signs. (FOR RENT; STAIRS.)

Ask for information about housing including location, number of and type of rooms, rent, deposit, and utilities. ("Where is the apartment?"; "How many rooms are there?"; "How much is the rent?")

Identify total amount due on monthly bills. (AMOUNT DUE; $35.87)

Arrange a time with the landlord or superintendent to make household repairs in person. ("Can you fix the furnace in the morning?")

Describe own housing situation, including cost and size and number of household members. ("My apartment is too small.")

Make simple arrangements to view housing in person. ("Can I see the apartment this afternoon?")

State housing needs and ask specific questions about cost, size, accessibility to transportation and community services and basic conditions for rental — date available, number of persons allowed, in person. ("When is the apartment available?"; "Where is the nearest bus stop?")

Make arrangements with the landlord to move in or out of housing, including return of deposit. ("I'd like to move in on June 19.")

Question errors of household bills in person. ("There's a mistake on my telephone bill. I didn't make these long-distance calls.")

Ask about and follow special instructions for using/maintaining common household equipment and facilities — defrosting the refrigerator, lighting the pilot, using laundry facilities. ("How do I turn on the heat?")

Ask about and follow special instructions on the use of an apartment or housing. ([Take out the garbage on Thursdays])

Ask to borrow basic tools and household items from a neighbor. ("Excuse me, can I borrow a hammer?")

Arrange for installation or termination of household utilities. ("I'd like to have a telephone installed as soon as possible.")

Question errors on household bills on the telephone. ("I have one phone. Why am I charged for two phones?")

Explain the exact nature or cause of a household problem. ("The bathroom sink is leaking. There's water all over the floor.")

Read classified ads and housing notices.

Read utility meters and bills.

Make complaints to and respond appropriately to complaints from neighbors or the landlord. ("Your dog barks too much. We can't sleep. Can you keep him quiet?")

Ask about and describe landlord/tenant responsibilities. ("The landlord has to pay for the gas.")

State needs and ask specific questions about housing or a rental agreement by telephone. ("Is the rental agreement for one year or for two years?")

Ask about and answer questions regarding a lease or rental agreements.

Read a non-simplified housing lease or rental agreement and fill it out with assistance.

SHOPPING

State basic food needs. ("I need rice.")

Ask the price of food, clothing, or other items in a store. ("How much is this coat?")

Read a limited number of basic store signs (IN, OUT, SALE)

State basic clothing needs. ("I need a coat.")

Read aisle numbers. (2B)

Differentiate sizes by reading tags. (S, M, or L; 8, 10 or 12.)

Read abbreviations for common weights and measures in a supermarket. (LB; QT)

Read common store signs. (IN, OUT, UP, DOWN, CASHIER)

Ask about and read signs for store hours. (OPEN, CLOSED; SAT. 9 a.m. — 12 p.m.)

Read expiration dates. (EXP. 4/4/84; SELL BY 4/8/82)

Request size and color for a specific item in simple terms. ("Do you have a small size?")

Ask for information about places to buy food/clothing/household items. ("Where can I buy rice?")

Ask for and follow simple directions to locate food/clothing in a store. ("Where are the coats?" [In Aisle 4A])

Ask for food using common weights and measures ("One pound of hamburger, please.")

Order and pay for food at a fast food restaurant. ("A hamburger and a Coke, please.")

Read prices and weights of various food items and determine the best buy by comparing. ($1.89/LB. $1.99/LB.)

Respond to cashier's questions concerning means of payment. ([Cash or charge?] ("Cash".)

Request a different size or price ("Do you have a bigger one?")

Ask for a receipt. ("Can I have a receipt, please?")

Express a need to return/exchange merchandise and state satisfaction/dissatisfaction with an item in terms of color, size, fit, etc. ("This is too big.")

Read supermarket/department store newspaper ads or use coupons for comparative shopping. (FLORIDA ORANGES, 5 LB. BAG $1.79).

Locate items in a supermarket/store by reading common section/department signs. (PRODUCE, HOUSEWARES)

Read a variety of store signs indicating sales or special prices. (REDUCED; TODAY ONLY)

Request a particular color or style of clothing. ("Do you have this in light blue?")

Ask about and follow oral instructions for care of clothing or read labels on clothing in symbols and words. ([Wash it in cold water,] "Can I put this in the dryer?")

Read names of different types of stores. (HARDWARE,

JEWELRY).

Ask about and understand basic information about store hours, products and prices over the telephone. ("Do you make keys?")

Read food labels and follow directions for preparing food.

Write a letter to question a bill.

Read consumer protection laws and product warranties.

TRANSPORTATION

Ask the amount of local bus or train fares. ("How much is a bus ticket?")

Read a limited number of symbols or transportation/pedestrian signs. (BUS STOP; WALK/DON'T WALK.)

Ask for a transfer. ("A transfer, please.")

Ask for a bus, train, or plane destination. ("Where does this bus go?")

Read signs indicating bus/train destinations and street names (MAIN STREET).

Ask for information about a location in an airport, bus or train station. ("Where is Gate 10?")

Respond to and ask basic questions about one's own or others departure/arrival times. ("When are you leaving?")

Respond to common requests.([Please move to the back of the bus.])

Ask when and where to get off or on a local bus/train station. ("I'm going to the post office . Where do I get off?")

Buy bus, train, or plane tickets. ("I'd like a one-way ticket to Chicago.")

Read common signs in an airport or bus/train station. (TO GATES 6-14; TICKETS).

Read common traffic and pedestrian signs. (ONE WAY; KEEP RIGHT; NO PARKING).

Ask where a bus/train is going, where it stops, and which buses/trains stop at a given stop. ("Which bus stops at Main Street and Second Avenue?")

Read an arrival/departure information board in an airport or bus/train station.

Read printed bus/train schedules.

Fill out a state driver's license application.

Ask for information in order to purchase a used car. ("What's the mileage?")

Answer a police officer's questions regarding a car accident or traffic violation.(["How fast were you going?"] ("55")

Fill out a car accident report.

Describe common car problems in need of repair. ("My car won't start.")

Ask and answer questions and read related to buying car insurance.

Get detailed long-distance travel information over the telephone such as schedules and costs. ("What's the cheapest way I can fly round-trip from New York to San Francisco?")

Part II — Additional Competencies Listed by area

Competencies listed from lowest to highest level of difficulty.

CLARIFICATION

Express a lack of understanding. ("I don't understand.")

Ask someone to repeat. ("Please repeat it again.")

Ask someone to speak slowly. ("Please speak slowly.")

Repeat something when asked to do so. ("My name is Tran.") [Could you repeat that?] "(My name is Tran.")

Ask the English word for something. ("What's this?")

Ask the meaning of something written in English. ("What's this?")

Verify the name of something by asking simple yes/no questions. ("Is this the Post Office?")

Ask for information or clarification using basic question words. ("How?"; "Go where?")

Give clarification in response to basic question words. ("Tung is not here." [Who?] "Tung.")

Ask someone to spell or write something. ("Can you write it for me?")

Ask about the meaning or the pronunciation of a word. ("What does _____ mean?"; "How do you say _____?")

Ask for clarification using a partial question with appropriate gestures. ([Go to the cafeteria.] "Go to...?")

Spell or write something for purposes of clarification.

Repeat instructions to verify comprehension. ([Go to Room 4.] ("Room 4?")

Identify which part of instructions or an explanation are not understood. ("I don't understand what to do after I put these away.")

Ask for clarification by giving alternatives. ("Fifteen or fifty?")

Rephrase one's own explanation/statement. ("He's not here." [What?] "He's absent.")

Respond to a listener's need for clarification of own speech by rephrasing. ("Take the box in the hall to the office." [What?] "There is a box in the hall. Take it to the office.")

Paraphrase complex ideas or difficult concepts.

DIRECTIONS

Ask for the location of common places within a building. ("Where is the bathroom?")

Ask for the location of a place. ("Where is the bus stop?")

Read, say, and copy numbers as used on streets and buildings.

Follow simple oral directions to a place. ([Turn right/left. Go straight.])

Respond to simple questions about a destination. ([Where are you going?] "To the bank.")

Follow a simple hand-drawn map to locate a place in an already familiar setting when directions are also given orally. ([Go one block. Turn left.])

State the location of own residence by giving the address and nearest streets, or by referring to familiar landmarks. ("I live near the hospital.")

Follow simple oral directions to places in a building. ([Upstairs; Third Floor; To Room 14A])

Give simple directions to a place. ("Turn right/left. Go to the third house.")

Identify own home and major streets or landmarks on a simplified map. ("I live on 22nd St.")

Find a place by following simple written directions. (GO TWO BLOCKS. TURN LEFT.)

Follow and give multiple-step directions to specific places within a building. ("Go to the second floor and turn right. It's the third door on the left.")

Use a map to find a place.

Give specific instructions in person to a place which is marked clearly on a map. ("Go north three blocks. Turn right on 10th Street. The Post Office is on the left.")

Write and follow simple directions to a place which are given over the telephone.

MONEY

Identify United States coins and bills by name and value. ("Dime"; "10 cents.")

Read prices on tags or signs. ($1.25)

Use money correctly to pay the total amount requested orally or in written form at a store, post office, vending machine, etc. ([That's $9.80])

Make or respond to a request for change. ("Do you have change?")

Make or respond to a request for specific coins. ("Do you have a dime?")

Read names of coins on coin-operated machines. (NICKELS, DIMES, QUARTERS)

When incorrect change is received, identify and request correct amount of change from a purchase. ("Excuse me, my change should be $5.00.")

Report problems in using coin-operated machines. ("I lost a quarter in the machine.")

Write information related to personal income on forms, such as employment and training applications.

PERSONAL IDENTIFICATION

Respond to basic questions regarding name, ID/Social Security number, country of origin, address, age, birthdate, and marital status. ([What's your name?"] "Sarem Nouan.")

Indicate which of own names are first, last and middle. [(What's your last name?] ("Tran.")

Spell, Read, and print own name.

Copy basic personal information, including name (first and last), ID/Social Security number, address, and age on a simplified form.

Present identification upon request. ([Can I see some identification?])·

State ability to speak a language other than English. ("I speak Lao.")

Write and read basic personal information including relationship, and age of family members.

Respond to questions about own ethnic group. ([Are you Hmong?] ("Yes.")

Spell own name, country of origin, and address when requested.

Respond to questions about own ability to speak, read and write English and any other language. ([Which languages do you know?] "I can speak Assyrian and Arabic.")

State the number of years of previous education or study of English. ([How many years did you go to school?] ("Eight.")

Give the names of familiar people. ([Who is your sponsor?]("Mr. John Doe.")

Fill out a simple form, including name, address, age, signature, country of origin, birthplace, marital status, sex, title (Mr., Mrs., Ms.)., citizenship, and maiden name.

State or write the name, relationship, and age of family members.

State or write own physical characteristics, including height, weight, color of hair, eyes.

Provide information about a sponsor, including the name, agency, and contact person, address, and telephone number. ("My sponsor is USCC ")

Describe self and members of immediate and extended family, giving details about background.

Fill out a variety of forms including - but not limited to credit applications, tax forms, medical forms, and school registration forms.

SOCIAL LANGUAGE

Introduce oneself using simple language. ("I'm Sarem.")

Give and respond to simple greetings and farewells. ([Hello. How are you?] "Fine, thanks. And you?")

Excuse oneself politely. ("Excuse me.")

State weather conditions in simple terms. ("It's cold.")

Answer simple questions about personal background and family. ([How many children do you have?"] "Three.")

State likes and dislikes using simple language. ("I like tea.")

Respond to simple questions about daily activities and weekly routines. ([What time do you stop working?] "5:00")

State general feelings in simple terms. ("I'm tired"; "I'm sad.")

Respond to common gestures such as handshaking, headshaking to indicate yes/no, beckoning, etc.

Initiate and respond appropriately to a variety of greetings and farewells in simple terms. ([Have a nice day.) ("Thanks. You too.")

Introduce family, friends, and co-workers using simple language. ("This is Somsy.")

State food and drink preferences in social conversations, using simple language. ([Do you want coffee?] "No, tea, please.")

Respond to simple questions about another's person's name and background. ([Who's that?] ("Ly.") [Where's she from?] ("Vietnam.")

Ask for assistance in simple terms. ("Can you help me?")

Thank someone for help or for a gift in simple terms. ("Thank you.")

Ask simple questions about daily activities and weekly routines. "(Do you work on Saturdays?")

Make and respond to invitations and offers in person using simple language. ([Do you want a ride home?] ("Yes, thank you.")

Ask permission to use or to do something. ("Can I smoke here?")

Give simple compliments about food, clothing, or housing. ("I like your watch.")

Ask simple questions about another person's name and background. ("Who's that?") [Tran] ("Where's he from?" [Vietnam])

Identify major United States holidays. ("New Year's Day"; "Thanksgiving"; etc.)

Give basic information about the journey from the native country to the United States. ("I went by boat to

Indonesia. I stayed in a refugee camp for two years.")

Suggest appropriate clothing/activities based on the weather. ("It's very cold. You should wear a hat.")

Talk about personal interests, recreation, or hobbies. ("I like to cook.")

Ask for information about some common practices on major American holidays in simple terms. ("What do people do on Thanksgiving?")

Thank someone for help or for a gift in a variety of ways. ("Thank you for the gift. It's very nice.")

Respond to and ask questions about personal background, weekend plans, recent experiences, weather, traffic, etc. ("What are you going to do this weekend? I'm going to a soccer game.")

Answer questions about differences between the native country and the United States in simple terms. ("In this country, my wife works. I take care of my children.")

Ask about the appropriateness of actions according to the customs/culture in the United States. ("Is it all right to wear my shoes in the house?")

Ask for or offer assistance. (I'm going to the supermarket. Can I get anything for you?")

Request advice about resolving personal problems. ("I had an accident. What should I do?")

Identify others by description and location rather than by name. ("The woman with the long hair and brown skirt"; "The man on the left.")

Decline an invitation or postpone a social engagement. ("I'm sorry. I'm busy tomorrow. Can we go shopping next Saturday?")

Initiate and maintain a conversation about movies, TV shows, sports events, and speakers/formal talks on most non-technical subjects.

Order a meal from a menu in a restaurant.

Respond to and make invitations over the telephone. ("Would you like to go shopping tomorrow?"; "Yes, I would.")

Get information about the weather, time, business hours, etc., from most recorded announcements.

Enter into ongoing social conversations on a variety of topics.

TELEPHONE

Note: While use of the telephone in basic survival situations is not expected until later in the teaching, instruction in emergency use of the telephone cannot be postponed until that time.

Identify the symbol or read the sign for a public telephone. (PHONE; TELEPHONE)

Read and be able to dial a limited list of telephone numbers such as those for a school, sponsor, or emergency. (911)

Identify oneself on the telephone when answering and when calling ("This is Tran.")

Request to speak to someone on the telephone. ("Tran, please.")

Ask for someone on the telephone. ("Is Tran there?")

Respond to a simple request to "hold" on the telephone.
([Please hold.])

When answering the telephone, locate the person requested or indicate that the person is not there, and take the name and telephone number of the caller when necessary. ("Yohanis isn't here.")

Respond appropriately when making or receiving a wrong number call. ("I'm sorry you have the wrong number.")

Make a long-distance call by direct dialing, or with the help of an operator.

Take a short telephone message. ("Dr. Smith called. Call him back at 10:00.")

Leave a short message. ("This is Tran. I'll call back at 9:00.")

Use the telephone book to find telephone numbers.

Use the telephone book or call information to get area codes, long distance rates, or telephone numbers not listed in the directory.

Respond appropriately to recorded messages and instructions. ([At the sound of the tone, leave your name and number.] "This is Tran. Please call me. My number is _____.")

Use the yellow pages of the telephone book to find specific types of businesses, products, and services.

Make and receive collect and person-to-person, operator assisted calls.

Use the telephone to make routine social plans.

Use the telephone to obtain detailed information about products, services, and entertainment.

TIME

Ask and answer basic questions about time, such as days, current months, yesterday/today/tomorrow. ([What month is it?] "February.")

Read clock time on the hour and half hour.

Read and write digital time on the hour, half hour and quarter hour. (10:15)

Read the days of the week.

Identify parts of the day — morning, afternoon, evening and night.

Name and read all the days of the week and the months of the year and their abbreviations.

Read and write dates when expressed in numbers; read and write months when expressed in words. (5/10/82; MAY 10, 1982.)

Read any time expressed in digital terms. (10:23 A.M.)

Ask and answer basic questions about days, months, and years.

Use a calendar.

Ask about and give dates when asked. ([When is your daughter's birthday?] "November 23rd.")

Write the date as requested on a variety of forms.

Ask and answer questions using general time phrases. ([When does school start?] "Next Monday." [When did you come to the U.S.?] "Last year.")

Read and write clock time. (A QUARTER AFTER TEN - 10:15; TWENTY MINUTES TO ELEVEN - 10:40)

Appendix B

Sequence of Skills - A Check List

Listed below are items that should be taught in sequence. The sequence suggested in any of the areas (structures, time, objects, etc.) is just that - suggested! You may find yourself teaching a structure in the intermediate level before something else, because that's what your student needs. That's perfectly all right. You're helping your student meet individual immediate needs. The progression helps give *you* some order. Use it to your **advantage**.

Structures[1]

BEGINNING

    Verbs - Simple present (I go. You go. He, she, it goes, etc.)
              Verb + "to be" + adjective (I am happy, etc.)
              Verb + "to be" + noun (I am a boy.)
              Present continuous (I am walking.)
    Questions - Information - What (about things)
                            Where (about places)
                            When (about time)
                            Who (about people)
                            How many/much **(about numbers or quantity)**
                            Why/because (about actions)
        Yes/No
            Simple present (Do you eat lunch at noon? Yes, I do.)
            Simple present "to be" (Are you a student? Yes, I am.)
            Present progressive (Are you going to the store? No, I'm not.)
        Choice questions
            Simple present (Do you walk or run? I run.)
            Present progressive (Is he running or walking? He's walking.)
    Pronouns - Personal (I, you, he, she, it, we, they)
                Possessive (mine, yours, his, hers, its, our, their)
    Adjectives - Possessive (my, your, his, her, its, our, their)
                Demonstrative (this, that, these, those)
  Prepositions of place (to, at, in, on, under, behind, near, etc.)
  Conjunctions (and, or)

INTERMEDIATE

    Verbs - Simple past (regular: I climbed; irregular: I sang; "to be": I was a fireman.)
              Future ("going to" + verb: I am going to sing. "will" + verb: I will run.)
    Questions - Information (see Beginning Level)
           Yes/No
            Simple past (Did I climb? Yes, I did.)
            Future (Am I going to eat? Yes, I am. Will we run? No, we won't.)
        Choice questions
            Simple past (Did he run or walk? He walked.)
            Future (Are we going to New York or San Francisco? We're going to New York.)
    Prounouns - Review personal and possessive from Beginning Level.
                Object (me, you, her, him, it, us, them)
    Adjectives - Possessive (see Beginning Level)
  Conjunctions (and, but, or)

[1]Adapted from *Guide to Learning Better English* by Lee Hitchock Lacy (International Student Exchange, Washington, D.C.)

ADVANCED

Verbs - Past continuous (I was sitting.)

Questions - Information (see Beginning Level)

　　　　Yes/No

　　　　　Past continuous (Was she sitting? Yes, she was.)

　　　　Choice questions (Were they sitting or climbing? They were climbing.)

Pronouns - Review personal and possessive from Beginning Level

　　　　Indefinite (somebody, someone, one, no one, nobody, etc.)

　　　　Relative (who, which, that)

Conjunctions (because, while, etc.)

Numbers/Prices[2]

1 - 10	10¢ - dime
Telephone numbers	25¢ - quarter
Some street numbers	ordinal numbers (first, second, third, etc.)
11 - 100	50¢ - half dollar
1¢ - penny	$1.00, $2.00, $5.00, etc.
5¢ - nickel	combination of dollars and cents ($2.36)

Time

hour (one o'clock, six o'clock)	quarter hour (1:15, quarter of four; fifteen before (to) seven)
noon, midnight	minutes after the hour (twenty past eight; 8:10)
half hour (1:30, 6:30)	minutes before the hour (ten of (before, to) one)

Months/Days

days of the week (Monday, Tuesday, etc.)

months of the year (January, February, etc.)

dates with numbers (May first or May 1, etc.)

Nouns

(Food, Clothes, Furniture, etc.)

countable nouns (those which can be used with numbers, singular or plural verbs - i.e. apple, orange, dress, suit, tie, table, chair, mirror, etc.)

uncountable nouns (those which cannot be used with numbers and take a singular verb - i.e. meat, butter, coffee, wool, clothing, darkness, daytime, rain, news, etc.)

[2]Adapted from a paper by Lutheran Immigration and Refugee Service, "The Early Days", 1980.

Appendix C

Citizenship

Many conversational English tutors will have students whose ultimate aim is attaining United States or Canadian citizenship. Most cities have citizenship classes, either in the public schools or run by community groups, and the student advanced enough to be working for citizenship should be studying in such classes. Your role as a conversational English tutor is important because the ability to speak, read, and write English is a basic requirement for U.S. or Canadian citizenship, in most cases, citizenship, with only a few exceptions.

A substantial part of your tutoring session for this type of advanced student should be spent on the material to be covered in the Naturalization Examination. It will be helpful to your student if you have some basic knowledge of the requirements for United States or Canadian citizenship.

U.S. Citizenship Requirements

The applicant seeking U.S. citizenship must:

1. Have five year's legal, permanent residence in the United States.
2. Be at least 18 years of age.
3. Be able to speak, read, write and understand simple English.
4. Have some knowledge of our form of government and of U.S. history.
5. Be of good moral character
6. Show understanding of, and belief in, the Constitution of the United States.

These are the exceptions to the basic requirements:

A foreigner married to a spouse (who has lived in the United States for three years) and who has been a U.S. citizen for at least three years, may have only three years residence in the United States to qualify for citizenship. However, the requirement to speak, read, and write English still stands.

A person over 50 years of age with 20 years or more of residence in the United States may become a citizen even though he or she cannot speak, read, or write English.

NATURALIZATION PROCEDURES

If the applicant meets the basic requirements, the steps toward citizenship are as follows:

1. Obtain an application (Form N-400) for citizenship, a fingerprint card, and a Biographic Information form from the nearest office of the Immigration and Naturalization Service, the clerk of a Naturalization Court, or a social service agency in the community. The application, fingerprint form, and Biographic iniformation form, must be filled out and mailed to the nearest Immigration and Naturalization Office. (Here is an opportunity for the tutor to help the student in this beginning step toward citizenship by explaining the questions in the above forms).

2. After an examination of the application, the applicant will be helped in filing a Petition for Naturalization in the Naturalization Court. There is a $50 fee for filing.

3. After the petition has been filed, the applicant must wait for not less than 30 days and will then be notified to appear before the Court for a final hearing. The judge does not ordinarily ask any questions of the applicant because the Naturalization Examiner has already done so, and merely informs the Judge that the applicant has been found qualified and should be made a citizen. The Applicant then takes an Oath of Allegiance to the United States.

This brief review of the steps to citizenship can be supplemented by the free pamphlet available from the U. S. Department of Justice, Immigration and Naturalization Service, entitled "Naturalization Requirements and General Information."

NATURALIZATION EXAMINATION

A big challenge for many people in obtaining citizenship is the Naturalization Examination, which is one part literacy (reading and writing English) and the other part history and government of the United States.

OATH OF ALLEGIANCE

You will want to explain and simplify much of the information on citizenship. For example, here is the Oath of Allegiance to the United States. As you read it, think to yourself how very difficult and confusing the words would be to you if English were not your native language:

"I hereby declare, an oath, that I absolutely and entirely renounce and abjure all allegiance and fidelity to any foreign prince, potentate, state, or sovereignty of whom or which I have heretofore been a subject or citizen; that I support and defend the Constitution and laws of the United States of America against all enemies, foreign and domestic; that I will bear true faith and allegiance to the same; that I will bear arms on behalf of the United States or perform noncombatant service in the Armed Forces of the United States when required by law; and that I take this obligation freely without any mental reservation or purpose of evasion; so help me God."

You might explain its meaning even more simply, in this manner:

As a citizen of only the United States, I promise to obey all the laws of this country. I will defend the United States against all its enemies. I will serve in the armed services of the U.S.A. or do noncombatant service, if required. I make this pledge of my own free will, as an oath before God.

Canadian Citizenship Requirements

There are seven requirements to becoming a Canadian citizen.:

1. *Legal entry* — you must have been lawfully admitted to Canada for permanent residence, i.e. as a landed immigrant.

2. *Age* — you must be 18 years of age or older to apply for yourself.

3. *Residence* — you must have lived in Canada for a total time of three years within the four years immediately before your application for citizenship.

This means that absences from Canada are allowed, so long as your time in Canada adds up to three years, but only the four years up to the day you apply for citizenship are considered. Within that time, the period of residence is calculated as follows:

one half day for each day in Canada before the date of becoming a landed immigrant, and one day for each day in Canada after the date of becoming a landed immigrant.

4. *Freedom from prohibitions* — you cannot receive citizenship or take the oath of citizenship (i) if you are considered to be a risk to Canada's security, (ii) if you are under a deportation order, (iii) if you are on probation or parole, (iv) if you are in prison, or (v) if you have been convicted of an indictable offence within the past three years. Time spent in prison or on probation or parole does not count towards a period of residence.

5. *Official language* — you must know either English or French, the official languages of Canada, well enough to make yourself understood in the community. Courses in English and French are available in many places from schools and community organizations.

6. *Knowledge of Canada* — you must have some knowledge of your rights and responsibilities as a Canadian citizen and of Canada's political system, geography and history. Information on these subjects is contained in "The Canadian Citizen" and "A Look at Canada", the free instructional pamphlets, which the Citizenship Court will give you.

7. *Oath of Citizenship* — finally, you take and sign this Oath of Citizenship

"I swear/affirm that I will be faithful and bear true allegiance to Her Majesty Queen Elizabeth the Second, Queen of Canada, Her Heirs and Successors, according to law and that I will faithfully observe the laws of Canada and fulfil my duties as a Canadian citizen".

Then you are a Canadian citizen.

There are Citizenship Courts and Offices in more than 30 cities across Canada. Consult the Government of Canada section of your phone book, or write to: Registrar of Canadian Citizenship, Department of the Secretary of State, Ottawa, Ontario K1A 0M5.

Appendix D

Glossary of Terms

ABE Adult Basic Education.

ACE Adult Continuing Education.

ALM Audio-lingual method. A behaviorist approach to teaching languages which relies heavily on oral repetition and drills.

Bilingual Education The teaching of subject matter (math,science, social studies, etc.) in the student's native language (usually Spanish in the United States), with concurrent education in English.

C.A.I. Computer Assisted Instruction.

Conversational English — Basic literacy, listening comprehension, and speaking skills.

EFL English as a Foreign Language.

ESL English as a Second Language.

G.E.D. General Equivalency Diploma.

Grammar Translation — A method of teaching languages by learning grammar rules and translating into any given native language.

L.E.P. Limited English Proficiency.

Linguistics — A science which systematically analyzes and describes a language as used by its native speakers.

Natural approach — The learning of a foreign language intuitively by using it in natural or real situations.

TEFL Teaching English as Foreign Language.

TESL Teachers of English as a Second Language.

TESOL Teachers of English to Speakers of Other Languages (the professional organization of ESL teachers - TESOL, 202 D.C. Transit Building, Georgetown University, Washington, D.C. 20057).

TOFEL A test of English as a foreign language. A score of between 500 and 600 is needed for foreign students wishing to enter most American colleges and universities. Test applications are available from the Educational Testing Service, P.O. Box 899, Princeton, N.J. 08541-0008.

Appendix E

Guidelines for Selecting a Conversational English Textbook

Ask yourself these questions as you look for an appropriate text for your Conversational English student.

METHOD
1. Is the approach consistent with your teaching method?
2. Is the approach student centered?
3. Is the approach varied?

SUBJECT MATTER
4. Is the subject matter of current interest?
5. Is cultural and other information up to date and accurate?
6. Is the subject matter varied and appropriate to the interests of adult students?

USE
7. Is the text easy to use?
8. Is the text flexible enough to be used in a variety of ways?
9. Is there a teacher's manual or preface which explains how the text can best be used?

FORMAT
10. Does the text provide plenty of review in subsequent lessons of newly introduced material?
11. Do exercies and activities lend themselves to use with one student, rather than requiring a group of students to be effective?
12. Do the exercises require the student to engage in a variety of activities?
13. Are there exercises that allow the student to engage in meaningful communication?

Appearance
14. Are the illustrations lifeless or realistic?
15. Is the print adequate, or too small?
16. Is the layout cluttered, or easy to look at?

CULTURAL STABILITY
17. Does the text avoid giving the impression that all Americans are white Anglo-Saxon Protestant?
18. Does the text avoid racist and sexist stereotypes, and is ethnic stereotyping avoided?

ILLUSTRATIONS
19. Are there clear illustrations that aim to help students understand new vobabulary and structure?
20. Do the illustrations show individuals of both sexes and different racial and ethnic groups?

BIBLIOGRAPHY

Abdel-Messin Daoud and Marianne Celce-Murcia, "Selecting and Evaluating a Textbook," in Marianne Celce-Murcia and Lois McIntosh, eds., **Teaching English as a Second or Foreign Language** (Rowley, MA.: Newbury House, 1979), pp. 302-307.

Mildred R. Donoghue and John F. Kunkle, **Second Languages in Primary Education** (Rowley, MA.: Newbury House, 1979), pp. 119-120.

* Developed by Andrea Osborne, Ph.D., LVA's ESL Consultant (1978-1983), and revised for the Third Edition (1986).

Appendix F

Informal Placement Test

This test has been adapted from that conceived and written by Alice Perlman, Supervisor of Instruction, Title III, Adult Basic Education Program, New York City Board of Education. It is a test for those with little or no ability to speak or understand English, and is meant to be a guide for the tutor rather than a formal test of ability. It can also be used to quickly place a student.

Directions for Administering
ESL Placement Tests

1. Prior to testing, obtain background information on the student: address, phone number, age, marital status, native country, etc. This should be recorded.
2. Administer the test in a room where you are alone with the student.
3. Read each question to the student, recording the appropriate response.
4. No interpretation or helpful gestures should be used.
5. Questions should be asked in natural speech. Questions may be repeated once. (After scoring, you may explain the meaning of the question.)
6. The student should answer in English if possible. A correct answer can be given in standard English or poor English. Standard English is concerned with structurally correct language, not with pronunciation. An answer in the student's native language is incorrect for our purposes. We are testing the student's ability to understand and respond in *English*.
7. As the tester, listen carefully to the student's responses. It is your responsibility to listen carefully and to be sensitive to the student's comprehension and responses.

Explanation of Test Levels

The results of this test will place students into one of four levels, quickly giving general categories for placement.

Level I tests the student's ability to understand and respond to simply constructed questions which are spoken. Little oral production is required.

Level II tests both listening comprehension and oral production of simple short statements.

Level III indicates the student is capable of production of simple discourse in English.

Level IV is achieved when the student understands ordinary discourse (for example, a radio talk show) and can orally produce compound and complex sentences with reasonable correctness.

Teaching Plans Indicated
By Test Results

As you interpret the results of the test, adopt your plans for teaching, according to the following charts:

	Conversation (Listening and Speaking)	Reading as Reinforcement	Independent Reading and Writing
Levels 0-1	X		
Level II	X	X	
Levels III-IV	X	X	X

INFORMAL PLACEMENT TEST
PRE-TEST

☐ ESL Level 0   ☐ ESL Level I   ☐ ESL Level II   ☐ ESL Level III   ☐ ESL Level IV

Student's Name _____ Date _____

Tester's Name _____

ESL Level 0 If the student is unable to understand or respond in English, or answers only one or two questions in Level I (in standard or poor English), the ESL Level is 0.

ESL Level I If the student answers three to five Level I questions correctly (in standard or poor English), the ESL Level is at least Level I. Continue testing with Level II questions to determine possible higher level ability. If the student answers two or fewer Level I questions correctly (in standard or poor English), the ESL Level is 0.

Questions:	Correct Answer (Standard English)	Correct Answer (Poor English)	Incorrect Answer
1. Hello! what's your name?	_____	_____	_____
2. What's your address?	_____	_____	_____
3. What country are you from?	_____	_____	_____
4. Are you working now?	_____	_____	_____
5. What month of the year is this?	_____	_____	_____

(Number of correct answers in Level I _____)

ESL Level II If the student answers three to five Level II questions correctly (in standard or poor English), the ESL Level is at least Level II. Continue testing with Levels III and IV questions to determine possible higher level ability. If the student answers two or fewer Level II questions correctly (in standard or poor English), the ESl Level is I.

Questions:	Correct Answer (Standard English)	Correct Answer (Poor English)	Incorrect Answer
1. How many years did you go to school in (native country)?	_____	_____	_____
2. Did you ever study English before?	_____	_____	_____
3. How do you (or your husband or children) get to work (or school)?	_____	_____	_____
4. If you can't meet with your tutor for a lesson what could you do? (or) If you have a headache, what would you do?	_____	_____	_____
5. (If your student is employed) What kind of work do you do? (If your student is not in the labor market) what do you like to do for fun?	_____	_____	_____

(Number of correct answers in Level II _____)

ESL Levels III and IV Encourage your student to answer in at least three sentences. If the answers are too brief, you can suggest, "Tell me more." If the student cannot give a three-sentence answer for any of the following questions the ESL Level is II. If the student gets one correct answer (three-sentences), the ESL Level is III. If the student gets two or more correct answers (three sentences each), the ESL Level is IV.

Questions:	Correct Answer (Standard English)	Correct Answer (Poor English)	Incorrect Answer
1. Why did you move to (present location)?	_____	_____	_____
2. How do you think studying English will help you?	_____	_____	_____
3. Tell me how you celebrate (one of student's native holidays, or a birthday)?	_____	_____	_____

(Number of correct answers in Levels III and IV _____)

INFORMAL PLACEMENT TEST
POST-TEST

☐ ESL Level I   ☐ ESL Level II   ☐ ESL Level III   ☐ ESL Level IV

Student's Name _____ Date _____

Tester's Name _____

ESL Level I If the student answers three to five Level I questions correctly (in standard or poor English), the ESL Level is at least Level I. Continue testing with Level II questions to determine possible higher level ability. It is assumed that a student can answer at least three Level I questions correctly (in standard or poor English) after tutoring.

Questions:	Correct Answer (Standard English)	Correct Answer (Poor English)	Incorrect Answer
1. What's your husband's (son's, mother's) name?	_____	_____	_____
2. Where does (he, she) (work, got to school, live)?	_____	_____	_____
3. Do you have a brother or sister?	_____	_____	_____
4. How long have you been in this country?	_____	_____	_____
5. What day is it today?	_____	_____	_____

(Number of correct answers in Level I _____)

ESL Level II If the student answers three to five Level II questions correctly (in standard or poor English), the ESL Level is at least Level II. Continue testing with Levels III and IV questions to determine possible higher level ability. If the student answers two or fewer Level II questions correctly (in standard or poor English), the ESl Level is I.

Questions:	Correct Answer (Standard English)	Correct Answer (Poor English)	Incorrect Answer
1. How did you travel to this country?	_____	_____	_____
2. How long have you been studying English?	_____	_____	_____
3. Do you speak any other languages beside (native language)?	_____	_____	_____
4. What's your favorite TV show?	_____	_____	_____
5. If you cut your finger, what would you do?	_____	_____	_____

(Number of correct answers in Level II _____)

ESL Levels III and IV Encourage your student to answer in at least three sentences. If the answers are too brief, you can suggest, "Tell me more." If the student cannot give a three-sentence answer for any of the following questions the ESL Level is II. If the student gets one correct answer (three-sentences), the ESL Level is III. If the student gets two or more correct answers (three sentences each), the ESL Level is IV.

Questions:	Correct Answer (Standard English)	Correct Answer (Poor English)	Incorrect Answer
1. Why did you move to (present location)?	_____	_____	_____
2. How do you think studying English will help you?	_____	_____	_____
3. Tell me how you celebrate (one of student's native holidays, or a birthday)?	_____	_____	_____

(Number of correct answers in Levels III and IV _____)

INDEX

For Muzzie

VIKING KESTREL
Viking Penguin Inc.
40 West 23rd Street
New York, NY 10010

First published in Great Britain by Walker Books Ltd
First American Edition
Published in 1985
Printed in Italy
1   2   3   4   5   89   88   87   86   85

ISBN 0-670-80806-7
Library of Congress catalog card number: 85-3327
(CIP data available)

Ben's Gingerbread Man

Niki Daly

VIKING KESTREL

Ben made a gingerbread man
at school. It smelled delicious,
but Ben didn't eat it. Instead
he held it carefully and
took it home.

At lunch-time Mom said,
"Why don't you eat your
gingerbread man?"
"He's too special," said Ben.

Ben made a bed for his gingerbread man.
He let the gingerbread man sleep
on a comfy chair.
"That's a safe place," Ben said.

But it wasn't!

CRUNCH! Mom sat down and
squashed the gingerbread man.

Ben was furious.

"I'm so sorry!" said Mom.

She offered Ben a gummy bear.

"I want my gingerbread
man!" wailed Ben.

Mom put the candy jar away.
She put on her apron and took out
her baking things.
"What are you doing?" sniffed Ben.
"You'll see," said Mom.

Mom stirred and then rolled out
the mixture. Ben licked the bowl.
It tasted of ginger!

Mom made four little gingerbread men.
One had raisin eyes and a raisin belly-button.
She put them in the oven to bake.

Mom gave Ben his
special gingerbread man.

Ben ate its legs.

He ate its arms.

He ate the gingerbread man's head.

Then he ate the gingerbread
man's belly-button!

"Where's your special gingerbread man?"
asked Mom.

"In my tummy," said Ben.

"Well, that's a safe place!" Mom laughed.
She gave Ben a hug.
They were friends again.